BRIGHT NOTES

STRANGE INTERLUDE BY EUGENE O'NEILL

Intelligent Education

Nashville, Tennessee

BRIGHT NOTES: Strange Interlude
www.BrightNotes.com

No part of this publication may be used or reproduced in any manner whatsoever without written permission, except in the case of brief quotations in critical articles and reviews. For permissions, contact Influence Publishers http://www.influencepublishers.com.

ISBN: 978-1-645421-22-1 (Paperback)
ISBN: 978-1-645421-23-8 (eBook)

Published in accordance with the U.S. Copyright Office Orphan Works and Mass Digitization report of the register of copyrights, June 2015.

Originally published by Monarch Press.
James J. Greene, 1965
2019 Edition published by Influence Publishers.

Interior design by Lapiz Digital Services. Cover Design by Thinkpen Designs.

Printed in the United States of America.

Library of Congress Cataloging-in-Publication Data forthcoming.
Names: Intelligent Education
Title: BRIGHT NOTES: Strange Interlude
Subject: STU004000 STUDY AIDS / Book Notes

CONTENTS

1) Introduction to Eugene O'Neill — 1

2) Introduction to Strange Interlude — 7

3) Conclusion — 29

4) Characters Analyses — 32

5) Structural Analysis — 48

6) Review of Criticism — 94

7) Essay Questions and Answers — 118

8) Selected Bibliography — 138

INTRODUCTION TO EUGENE O'NEILL

EARLY LIFE

Eugene O'Neill was born in a Broadway hotel on October 16, 1888. His father was a popular actor of romantic melodrama and Eugene's first seven years were spent in the larger towns all over the United States. The success of the *Count of Monte Cristo*, in which his father played the lead, kept the family engaged in almost continuous road tours. From the age of seven to thirteen he attended boarding schools. In 1902 he was sent to Betts Academy at Stamford and the autumn after his graduation he entered Princeton. Although his parents were Catholic, and he had been in and out of parochial schools from an early age, by the time he entered Princeton he had left the Church and never returned to it.

DISCONTENT WITH COLLEGE

In June of 1903 he was dismissed from Princeton, supposedly for throwing a beer bottle through a window of President Wilson's house. He could have returned the following year, but he had become bored with college and left to become a secretary in a New York mail-order house, the first in a long series of jobs he held before settling down to write.

YEARS OF WANDERING

In 1909 he married Kathleen Jenkins, a union that ended in divorce in 1912. In the same year he went on a gold-prospecting trip to Honduras. He had been reading Jack London, Kipling and Conrad, and we can see in the many journeys of his youth a desire to lead the rugged life of adventure that those writers took as their central **theme**. In 1910 he shipped on a Norwegian barque for Buenos Aires where he worked at some odd jobs, but ended up, in his own words, "a bum on the docks." In 1911, after a trip to Africa on a cattle steamer, he returned to New York where he lived at "Jimmy the Priest's," a waterfront dive which provided the setting for the first act of *Anna Christie*. After a last voyage to England he found himself on a train to New Orleans following a wild party. His father was playing there in the perennially popular *Monte Cristo*. He refused to give his son a handout, but did give him a part in the play. At the close of the season the O'Neills returned to their summer home in New London, Connecticut, where Eugene worked as a cub reporter on the *Telegraph*.

HIS DESIRE TO WRITE

In December of 1912 O'Neill entered a tuberculosis sanatorium. Weakened by years of irregular living, his health had broken down. During his fifteen month convalescence he first felt the urge to write. When he left the sanatorium he was a man with a purpose. To rebuild his health he disciplined himself to a life of exercise and hard work. In the next sixteen months he wrote eleven one-act plays, two long plays, and some poetry. He read omnivorously, in his own words "the Greeks and Elizabethans - practically all the classics - and of course all the moderns."

FIRST PLAYS

In the fall of 1914 he went to Harvard to take Professor George Baker's famous course in playwriting. In the same year his father financed the publication of his first book, *Thirst and Other One-act Plays*. Several plays in *Thirst* take men against the sea as their **theme**. O'Neill's classic statement of his **theme** is in the so-called Glencairn group, a sequence of one-act plays dealing with the tramp steamer Glencairn. The group consists of *The Moon of the Caribbees*, *Bound East for Cardiff*, *The Long Voyage Home* and *In the Zone*. In these plays man is shown in conflict with nature, which is indifferent to his suffering and inevitable doom. In his early naturalism O'Neill was deeply indebted to Jack London.

FIRST SUCCESS

In 1916 the Provincetown Players put on *Bound East for Cardiff*. It was O'Neill's first play to be acted. The Players were a group of Greenwich Village journalists, writers and painters who were interested in rejuvenating the American theater. In 1917–18 he had three plays published in *Smart Set*, a magazine of protest against the self-satisfied middle class, whose editors, H. L. Mencken and George Jean Nathan, were already known as literary critics. The production of *Beyond the Horizon* in 1920 brought O'Neill his first Pulitzer Prize, and from then until his death no one seriously questioned that he was the leading American playwright of his generation. In 1918 he had married Agnes Boulton Burton, and now, riding the wave of success, he had great faith in the future. However, he resolved he would never sell out to success. His father had felt that the temptation of easy money to be had from a play such as *Monte Cristo* had ruined his chances of becoming a fine actor. O'Neill resolved he would remain true to his dream and work to express the truth he had in him.

DISILLUSIONMENT

In spite of his remarkable success, O'Neill was convinced that bad fortune was hounding him. Throughout his life, except for brief periods, he had the feeling that man is at the mercy of mysterious forces beyond his control. He began to look back with nostalgia upon his seafaring days, and longed to be on the move again.

FINANCIAL SUCCESS

In the fall of 1920 *The Emperor Jones* was staged in London, Paris, Berlin, Tokyo and Buenos Aires, laying the foundation for O'Neill's international reputation. One year later *Anna Christie* opened in New York and brought him his second Pulitzer Prize. In 1922 *The Hairy Ape* was a success. It dramatized the idea that man has lost his old harmony with nature and is out of place in the modern, technological world. Late in 1922 O'Neill was making $850 a week in royalties. He bought a farm at Ridgefield, Connecticut, and settled down to live in landed elegance as his father had always desired to do.

HIS PESSIMISM

However, O'Neill could not settle down and two years later he was living in Bermuda and working on the idea for *Mourning Becomes Electra*. His idea of man at the mercy of mysterious forces had broadened through his reading of Freud, a German psychologist (1856–1939), Nietzsche, a German ethical writer who detested Christianity (1844–19000), and Schopenhauer, a German philosopher of the romantic period (1788–1860). From Freud he took the idea of man trapped by his unconscious sexual desires. Schopenhauer's pessimistic philosophy reinforced the naturalistic determinism that had been fostered by his reading of *London and Conrad*, and his own erratic life. From Nietzsche he took a joyous acceptance of despair as the only sane attitude for a man faced with an indifferent universe.

HONORED FOR HIS WORK

In 1926 he received the degree of Doctor of Literature from Yale University. Although at the height of his career, his personal life was a shambles. The following year he left his wife and two children to court Carlotta Monterey, the actress who had starred in *The Hairy Ape*. In 1928 *Strange Interlude* won a third Pulitzer Prize for him. Eugene and Carlotta took a whirlwind trip around the world and settled in a French chateau where he finished *Mourning Becomes Electra*. The play was presented in New York in October of 1931 and was immediately hailed as his masterpiece. Joseph Wood Krutch wrote that "it may turn out to be the only permanent contribution yet made by the twentieth century to dramatic literature."

AWARDED NOBEL PRIZE

From 1932 to 1936 O'Neill lived on an island off the coast of Georgia. The only successful play he wrote during this period was *Ah, Wilderness!*, the only comedy he ever composed. The play ran for 289 performances and brought O'Neill $75,000.

In November of 1936 he moved to Oregon with plans to write a cycle of plays designed to tell the story of the United States from the early 1700s. In the same month he became the first American playwright to receive the Nobel Prize.

HIS LAST WORK

During the latter part of his life only a few O'Neill plays were produced. In 1941 he completed the autobiographical *Long Day's Journey Into Night* which was first staged in 1956, three years after his death. It won his fourth Pulitzer Prize. His vision of life had not changed and the characters are unable to control the dark forces that shape their destinies. *The Iceman Cometh* was staged in 1946. It was an enormous success, but the play is uncompromisingly nihilistic in its philosophy. He suggests that man's urge toward the unattainable is his only justification, but what the unattainable is he can never know. O'Neill died in 1953 at the age of sixty-five. No one doubted that he was the greatest playwright America had produced.

STRANGE INTERLUDE

INTRODUCTION

Eugene O'Neill, the brooding, lonely artist whose memory haunts the contemporary theater, represents to many America's only major playwright, the only dramatist we have produced who can be ranked among the great figures of the European theater. There are, to be sure, eloquent and powerful voices who will deny such stature to O'Neill. Aware of O'Neill's high seriousness and artistic integrity, many of these same voices, while arguing vigorously against the greatness of the man's achievement, admit, sometimes grudgingly, his influence upon the American theater, since, as a result of his efforts, he has earned for the American playwright, in the words of one critic, "the right to be as serious as he wants to be and to aim as high as he can." One fact, in any case, seems certain at this point in time. Eugene O'Neill, whose prolific and uneven pen produced scores of plays, many of which have been produced all over the world, is a figure who cannot be ignored.

It seems natural to ask who this man was, this man whose life and works continue to be the center of heated controversy. It is, of course, a delicate, risky business to attempt a correlation between the life and the artistic work of any author. Although there is an inevitable relationship, a mutual influence, existing between the artist and his art, the nature of the relationship varies from person to person and remains, in the final analysis, mysterious and unapproachable. In the case of a man like Eugene O'Neill, however, it is especially tempting to try to see the man through his works, and vice versa, since so many of his plays drew so openly and unashamedly upon the materials of the author's life. O'Neill himself once remarked, "I have never written anything which did not come directly or indirectly from some event or impression of my own. ..." It is precisely for this reason, however, that we must be cautious about naively reading any of the plays as simple autobiographical statements. Art, after all, remains distinct from life, and between the lived experience and the play the shaping, transforming hand of the artist must always intervene.

Without pretending, then, to shed any special light on any of the plays, we might proceed to an examination of Eugene O'Neill's life, a life that was in its own way as elusive and as tragic as any of his plays. The facts of O'Neill's life - or at least most of them - are easily come by and are a matter of record, and even though the meaning of a man's life is much more than the sum of its factual parts, the data should be noted.

Life: Eugene Gladstone O'Neill was born on October 16, 1888, in New York City. He was the second son of Ella Quinlan O'Neill and James O'Neill, both of whom were devout and loyal Roman Catholics. The elder O'Neill was also an actor, one of the best known and most successful of his day. James O'Neill's chief contribution to the American theater, aside from his son Eugene, was to travel the length of the land giving endless performances as the star in that swashbuckling melodrama, *The*

Count of Monte Cristo. Towards the end of his life he is reported to have been bitter over his own rejection of artistic creativity and growth for the sake of financial reward.

Early Influences: To those interested in charting the forces "that shape our lives, rough hew them how we will," Eugene O'Neill's parentage and childhood environment are obviously of great significance. Nursed in the stage wings of countless theaters and living almost literally in dressing rooms during much of his childhood, the man who was to become America's major playwright breathed the air of the American theater from infancy onward. The theater was a part of his being, his "normal" surroundings, virtually from the moment of his conception. This by no means implies that he was determined or destined to become a playwright, but his early parental environment does suggest a possible source of his choice of the theater for his life's work.

O'Neill's crucially important decision to write for the stage cannot, of course, be explained quite so simply. The fact is that James O'Neill's son disliked what he saw of the American theater at that time, had contempt for its frivolity and superficiality, and strongly disapproved of the play which brought his father fame and profit. It is possible, in any event, that Eugene O'Neill's assault upon the American stage was to some extent a response to the shoddiness of that stage. To carry this speculation a step further, one might even see O'Neill's rebellion against the theatrical traditions embodied in his father as a rebellion against the father himself. It is well known that the relationship between father and son was characterized by misunderstanding, hostility, and alienation. As Eugene himself put it years later, "My early experience with the theater through my father really made me revolt against it."

Loss Of Faith: The other major source of parental influence upon the young O'Neill was, in an equally complicated way, his parents' Roman Catholicism. One dimension of Eugene O'Neill's rejection of the world into which he had been born was his abandoning the faith of his fathers, reportedly at the age of thirteen. The youth who rejected the God of Catholicism became the playwright who, by his own admission, was haunted by the need to seek a replacement for that God. In phrases that echo one of his favorite philosophers, Nietzsche, an older O'Neill was later to write of "the death of an old God and the failure of science and materialism to give any satisfying new one for the surviving primitive religious instinct to find a meaning for life in, and to comfort its fears of death with. It seems to me anyone trying to do big work nowadays must have this subject behind all the little subjects of his plays or novels." There was some speculation, after the production of *Days Without End* in 1934, that O'Neill had regained the lost faith of his youth. When the question was put to him directly, O'Neill answered, "Unfortunately, no."

It is difficult and perhaps ultimately impossible to trace with any certainty the influences that shape the life and work of a man. It seems reasonably clear, however, that the early parental influence upon O'Neill remained a major factor in his becoming a dramatist in the first place and a powerful, continuing force at work upon the plays he wrote. It is hardly without significance that in a great many of O'Neill's major works the domestic setting and familial struggles are at the center of his dramatic probing.

The crucial first seven years of his life O'Neill spent on tour with his father's acting company. His mother, by his own account, "had rather an aversion for the…stage in general." For the next several years the young O'Neill attended boarding schools, Catholic and non-sectarian. After graduation in 1906 from Betts Academy in Connecticut, he enrolled the following fall in Princeton University. His academic career was brief. He left Princeton at the end of his freshman year, having been suspended, without taking the final examinations. According to one widespread report - the product of George Jean Nathan's myth-making imagination - the suspension was the result of O'Neill's having hurled a beer bottle through one of President Wilson's windows. (The legend does not specify whether the window in the college president's house was open or whether the bottle was full.) There followed a brief spell as a clerk in a New York business with which his father had connections, his marriage in 1909 to Kathleen Jenkins, the birth of a son, Eugene Jr., in 1910, and his divorce in 1912.

The Sea Voyages: In the latter part of 1909 O'Neill set out on the first of his many restless wanderings, geographical and spiritual. This one took him to Honduras, prospecting for gold. There is no record that any was discovered. We next hear of him the following year, when he joined his father's company, touring with it for several months as assistant manager. Dissatisfied with the work, he left the company at the close of the season and signed on as a seaman on a merchant ship leaving for Buenos Aires. This experience and others leading directly from it were to have profound effects upon his future writing.

After a sixty-five-day trip to Argentina, the young seaman disembarked and began to roam the wharves, melting into the dockside life of the sailors and stevedores. He became, in his own words, "a bum on the docks in fact."

Lure Of The Sea: The natural lure of the sea for O'Neill, an attraction which was later to find a poignant, almost mystical expression in many of his plays, was undoubtedly nourished by the young O'Neill's admiration for Conrad's fiction as well as by his devotion to the life and works of another of his literary heroes, Jack London. His brief but intense career as a seaman (of which his father, incidentally, strongly approved) was, however, more than simply a desire to emulate the he-man heroics of Jack London. It was also clearly an escape from a life, an atmosphere, which had begun to suffocate him.

In Buenos Aires O'Neill worked at several odd jobs and then signed on once more for a voyage, this time to Africa on a cattle steamer. He never actually set foot in Africa, however, and signed on for the return voyage to South America, where he lived, in his own words, "on the beach," to all intents and purposes a derelict.

The life O'Neill lived during this period, a life which so deeply influenced so many of the plays he was later to write, had nothing to do with a young man's artificial search for experiences later to be exploited for artistic purposes. At that time the restless O'Neill had in no sense committed himself to a writing career. His first book of published plays, though, *Thirst and Other One-Act Plays*, which was issued in 1914, contains work which obviously came directly out of the experiences of his sea voyages. Some indication of the deep-seated impact of the sea upon the playwright's imagination may be gleaned from the fact that, of his forty-four published plays, thirteen of them are set partially or wholly aboard ship, and in at least six others the sea is an important element in the drama.

Back To The States: O'Neill returned to the states financially impoverished but enriched with a treasury of experience against which he was to draw throughout his literary career. He took up residence near the New York waterfront in a strange hotel-saloon called Jimmy the Priest's. (The proprietor was so named because, thin and ascetic looking, he reminded his patrons more of a priest than of a bartender.) There for the sum of three dollars a month one was entitled to the use of a vermin-infested room.

Lacking the three dollars, patrons were allowed to sleep with their heads on the tables in Jimmy's back room. According to O'Neill's later reminiscences, the hovels inhabited by the tramps in Gorki's plays were "ice cream parlors" by comparison. O'Neill was later to use this Fulton Street dive as the setting for *Anna Christie*, in which the saloon keeper is named Johnny the Priest. He resurrected his memory of this down-and-out existence once again in one of his last works, *The Iceman Cometh*: this play is set in a losers' pub which is a cross between Jimmy the Priest's and another hell-hole in Greenwich Village which the playwright frequented a few years after leaving Jimmy's. O'Neill once remarked of his experiences at Jimmy the Priest's, "I learned…not to sit in judgment on people." It might be pointed out in passing that understanding as distinct from judgment of people is a vital precondition for one who would write.

During this period O'Neill ventured uptown several times to attend performances by the Irish Players, who had temporarily abandoned their home base, the Abbey Theater in Dublin, for a tour of this country. One of the plays which impressed O'Neill most was, not surprisingly, John Millington Synge's stark, lyrical tragedy about men destroyed by the sea, *Riders to the Sea*.

Actor And Reporter: Shortly after this we find O'Neill joining his father's troupe in New Orleans as an actor. By his own admission he was one of the world's worst actors. He remained on tour with the *Monte Cristo* play for several months, during which time he was drinking heavily, and then in 1912 he journeyed to New London, the O'Neill summer residence, to begin work as a reporter on the New London *Telegraph*. His career as a reporter was unspectacular and short-lived, but during this five-month period he contributed some verse to the paper and began turning over in his mind the idea of writing plays.

TB Sanitarium: The years of dissipated living took their inevitable toll, and in December of 1912 O'Neill entered a sanitarium in Fairfield County, Connecticut, with a case of tuberculosis. He later commented on this six-month stay of enforced quiet and rest, "It gave me time to think about myself and what I was doing - or, rather, wasn't doing. I got busy writing one-act plays." During this time he read two works which deeply affected him: Dostoyevsky's *The Idiot* and, more importantly, Strindberg's play *The Dance of Death*. The play by the great Swedish playwright, whose work came to constitute the chief literary influence upon O'Neill's writing, is a merciless exposure of the corrosive, destructive cruelty systematically practiced against each other by the members of a family bound together in a fatal love-hate relationship. Given the circumstances of O'Neill's own tragic family situation, one can well imagine the powerful response such a play must have evoked in the sensitive young TB patient.

Years later, in his speech accepting the Nobel Prize awarded him in 1936, O'Neill spoke of his debt to "that greatest genius of all modern dramatists... August Strindberg." "It was reading his plays," O'Neill said, "when I first started to write...that, above all else, first gave me the vision of what modern drama could be, and first inspired me with the urge to write for the theater myself." We must remember that when O'Neill began to write, the American theater totally lacked anything even remotely comparable in seriousness and artistic achievement to a European drama which had already produced Hauptmann, Ibsen, Turgenev, Tolstoy, Chekhov, Strindberg, Gorki, Shaw and Synge.

Baker's Harvard Seminar: After leaving the sanitarium in 1913, O'Neill settled down in earnest to the writing of plays. His health was still fragile, and he lived in New London during 1913–14, devoting himself fully to writing one-act plays. In the fall of 1914 he enrolled in Professor Baker's famous playwriting seminar at Harvard, English 47. O'Neill has stated that the plays he wrote for Baker were "rotten." Although the Harvard professor rejected O'Neill's earlier *Bound East for Cardiff* as "not a play," Baker did impart something of inestimable value to the fledgling playwright: "He helped us to hope - and for that we owe him all the finest we have in memory of gratitude and friendship."

Greenwich Village: In 1915 O'Neill returned to New York. He took up with a group of down-and-outers and also plunged into the Bohemian life of Greenwich Village. Here he formed friendships with people like John Reed, the socialist writer, and others whose interests centered on revolt and various forms of socialism, radicalism and anarchy. One of the bars in which O'Neill did a good deal of his heavy drinking at this time was a place known as the Hell Hole. Here he met the anarchist hobo-intellectual, Terry Carlin, who served as the model for Larry Slade in *The Iceman Cometh*. Many of the other characters he encountered at this time were also to have their fictional counterparts as habitués of Harry Hope's saloon in that same play.

Provincetown: Finding himself unable to write, O'Neill temporarily abandoned the hectic Village life and in 1916 went to Provincetown, Massachusetts. Here in the seclusion of Cape Cod, accompanied by the intellectual hobo, Carlin, he lived, swam, and wrote on virtually "nothing a year." This move to Provincetown was to prove one of the decisive factors in his career as a playwright, for it led directly to his getting his work produced on a stage; without such an outlet, of course, a working playwright is, to all intents and purposes, artistically dead.

The Players: In the summer of 1915, a year before O'Neill's arrival in Provincetown, a group of Greenwich Villagers, dissatisfied with the recently established Washington Square Players, had formed a new group known as the Provincetown Players in the very place where O'Neill had taken up his abode. They had converted an abandoned fish warehouse into a theater of sorts and had determined to stage whatever plays they could find which seemed to have merit. The Wharf Theater, as their new establishment was named, represented a total rejection of the frivolous commercialism which then dominated every segment of the American theater. They were, in short, dedicated to raising American drama to the level of art. To accomplish this they proposed to stage original works written by themselves and other American playwrights, as well as translations of European plays.

First Play Produced: The summer of 1916 was their second season at Provincetown, and it was during this summer that Eugene O'Neill and the Provincetown Players discovered each other, surely one of the most significant encounters in the history of the American theater. At the urging of his crony, Terry Carlin, O'Neill one evening read one of his plays, *Bound East for Cardiff*, to the group. George ("Jig") Cook, one of the guiding lights of the Players, was, along with the rest, struck by the work, and they immediately decided to stage it that summer. It was in this fashion that a Eugene O'Neill play first got onto the boards, the only place where a play can have its real existence. The cast included Jig Cook, John Reed, and O'Neill himself, who played the Mate, a one-line, walk-on role. The playwright later recalled this crucial event in his career: "It's rather a curious coincidence that my first production should have been on a wharf in a sea town.... *Bound East for Cardiff*...was laid on shipboard, and while it was being acted you could hear the waves washing in and out under the wharf."

Playwrights' Theater: At the end of the 1916 summer season, the group returned to New York, decided to establish themselves on a year-round, permanent basis, rented the ground floor of a brownstone at 139 MacDougal Street, converted it into a theater and christened it, at O'Neill's suggestion, The Playwrights' Theater. O'Neill remained associated with the group, continuing to drink heavily and to write plays for their stage. In the fall of 1916 the Provincetown Players re-staged *Bound East for Cardiff* and thus provided O'Neill with his New York debut as a dramatist. The playwright later remarked of this whole experience, "If I hadn't had the Provincetown Theater, I would have had to write commercial plays."

Eugene O'Neill, although a published and now a produced playwright, was still earning nothing from his writings and was forced to live on the one dollar a day dole provided him by his father. It was not until 1917th at he began earning a small income of royalties from some of his published plays. He continued writing, however, and attending rehearsals of his plays. (Throughout his life he rarely, if ever, went to a public performance of any of his plays.) All of this early work has about it that overwhelming, tragic sense of fate crushing man which was to characterize the plays he wrote throughout his life - with the notable exception of *Ah, Wilderness*! The elder O'Neill once complained to his son during these early years, "My boy, why don't you write pleasanter plays?"

Return To Provincetown: O'Neill, still feeling the need for seclusion in order to write, returned to Provincetown in 1917. Here he completed four plays: *Ile*, *Moon of the Caribbees* (his own favorite among all his one-acters), *The Long Voyage Home*, and *In the Zone*. During the summer of 1917 he began work on *Beyond the Horizon*, his first full-length play to be produced.

By 1917, then, O'Neill had committed himself to his life's work. His career as a playwright was launched fully, if a bit shakily. A great deal of loneliness, hard work, and hardship still faced him before he was to achieve recognition. Even after fame and success had come to him, his life continued to be dogged by suffering and tragedy.

Mencken And George Jean Nathan: At the conclusion of the 1917 summer season, he accompanied the Provincetown group back to New York. It was then that the young playwright first formed another personal association that was to provide him with what he greatly needed at this time - and in fact throughout his career - encouragement about his work. H. L. Mencken, the bad boy of American letters, was then conducting his vitriolic campaign against the "booboisie" in the pages of his magazine *The Smart Set*. O'Neill, not thinking of publication, decided to ask Mencken and the magazine's drama critic for an evaluation of his work. He submitted several of his plays for their opinion and, much to his delight and surprise, they liked them so much that, contrary to their practice, they decided to print three of the plays: *The Long Voyage Home*, *Ile*, and *Moon of the Caribbees*. Nathan, who had been urging the merits of European dramatists such as Ibsen and Strindberg, now took up the cudgels for the relatively unknown American dramatist. O'Neill was beginning to attract attention.

In October of 1917 one of O'Neill's plays, *In the Zone*, was produced by the Washington Square Players. The staging was more professional than the work of the earnest but more amateurish Provincetown Players at the Playwrights' Theater. This time the New York drama critics were in attendance (at the Playwrights' Theater they had to pay their own way) and were generally enthusiastic about O'Neill's play. The author even managed to earn a little money from this production.

Second Marriage: Once again O'Neill, tiring of Greenwich Village life, sought out the solitude of Provincetown, but this time he was accompanied by Agnes Boulton, who shortly thereafter (April, 1918) became the second Mrs. O'Neill. This marriage produced two children, Shane and Oona, who later married Charlie Chaplin. (O'Neill's son by his first marriage, Eugene Jr., taught Greek at Yale for a while and ended his life by suicide.)

O'Neill continued to write one-act plays for the Provincetown Players and completed work on his first full-length play, *Beyond the Horizon*. With the help of George Jean Nathan, O'Neill was able to secure a producer who agreed to stage the play, but it did not hit the boards until 1920. He had written several other full-length plays but, dissatisfied with them, he had destroyed them. Life continued to be a struggle, and, interrupted by periodic bouts of alcoholism, O'Neill continued to fight against the despair which throughout his life threatened to engulf him. He worked at a furious pace on the writing, publishing, and producing of his plays. He once told an interviewer, a propos of *The Straw*, a short play based on his experiences at the tuberculosis sanitarium, "My whole idea is to show the power of spiritual help even when a case is hopeless." This indomitable sense of hope in the midst of hopelessness was what enabled O'Neill to survive and to create. His own inner anguish, which he carried with him to the end of his life, was only temporarily relieved by his drinking. The memories and psychic scars inflicted by a hostile, often indifferent, always domineering father, a drug-addicted mother, and an alcoholic, totally self-destructive older brother always remained and were relieved neither by alcohol nor by the many love affairs and the three marriages into which he entered. Concerning his early drinking, about which much has been written, O'Neill commented:

"Altogether too much damn nonsense has been written since the beginning of time about the dissipation of artists. Why, there are fifty times more real drunkards among Bohemians who only play at art, and probably more than that among the people who never think about art at all. The artist drinks, when he drinks at all, for relaxation, forgetfulness, excitement, for any purpose except his art. You've got to have all your critical and creative faculties about you when you're working. I never try to write a line when I'm not strictly on the wagon. I don't think anything worth reading was ever written by anyone who was drunk or even half-drunk when he wrote it. This is not morality, it's plain physiology."

Around this time O'Neill lost interest in political and social causes. "Time was," he said, "when I was an active socialist, and after that, a philosophical anarchist. But today I can't feel that anything like that really matters."

In 1918 The Playwrights' Theater moved into more spacious quarters a few doors away, at 133 MacDougal Street. Early in 1919 O'Neill began work on the play that was eventually to be known as *Anna Christie*, and he also saw seven of his short plays through publication. It was characteristic of O'Neill that throughout his career he was always simultaneously working on several projects. His artistic energy was boundless.

Broadway Debut: On February 3, 1920, *Beyond the Horizon* finally opened in New York's Morosco Theater. O'Neill's Broadway debut was, ironically, the result of sneaking his play in the side door. The only way he could get the play staged was to have it played at matinees four days a week in the same theater (and by the same cast) at which Elmer Rice's *For the Defense* was the stellar evening attraction. The critics, in general, responded favorably to O'Neill's first full-length play. O'Neill's father and mother attended the premiere, and the old actor, whose theatrical star had fallen, was deeply moved by his son's work.

He said to him after the performance, "Are you trying to send the audience home to commit suicide?" The play was awarded the Pulitzer Prize, the first of four O'Neill was to receive. When *Beyond the Horizon* was revived in 1924, Joseph Wood Krutch, the young drama critic for *The Nation*, wrote that O'Neill had "come nearer than any other American to writing Tragedy." A new era, in which serious drama could command attention in the American theater, had arrived. Professor Baker, O'Neill's old Harvard teacher, analyzed the new situation: "A public which heartily welcomes *Beyond the Horizon* is not the old public. It seems now as if there really were in New York an audience large enough to make successful any kind of drama worthy of attention." Writing in retrospect in 1936, O'Neill himself gave the credit for creating this new audience to the Washington Square Players and the Provincetown Players. "These groups," he said, "helped make it possible to present serious dramas."

It was at this time that O'Neill became less interested in one-acters and began to devote his major efforts to longer plays. He began, in fact, to envision those really big, sprawling, dramatic works for which he was to become famous or notorious, depending on one's point of view. He saw himself in 1920, at the age of thirty-two, as just beginning to grow, and he looked forward, despite his saturnine view of life, to a future of great productivity. Writing to George Jean Nathan, he made his act of artistic faith in these words:

"I will not 'stay put' in any comfortable niche and play the leave-well-enough-alone game. God stiffen it, I am young yet and I mean to grow! And in this faith I live: That if I have the 'guts' to ignore the megaphone men and what goes with them, to follow the dream and live for that alone, then my real significant bit of truth, and the ability to express it, will be conquered in time - not tomorrow nor the next day nor any near, easily-attained period, but after the struggle has been long enough and hard enough to merit victory."

The Greenwich Village Theater: The years 1920–22 were very fertile ones for O'Neill. During that period New York stages were graced with no fewer than eight of his plays. In 1920, in addition to *Beyond the Horizon*, *The Emperor Jones* was staged in a New York theater and was received enthusiastically. This play, which introduced to the American theater new techniques associated with European expressionism, has remained one of the most popular and artistically successful works in the O'Neill canon. It brought the Provincetown Players their first truly widespread recognition. In 1923 O'Neill, together with Kenneth MacGowan and the famous scenic designer, Robert Edmond Jones, took over and operated for several years another small theater devoted to high quality drama, the Greenwich Village Theater.

By the time he was thirty-five, O'Neill had established himself as America's most prominent playwright. He was a success, a celebrity, and yet, as ever, he continued to shun the crowds, to avoid the public rituals which American society so frequently forces upon its cultural deities. O'Neill was still very much his own man, still cherishing the privacy and quiet he felt to be essential to his writing. He was convinced that his career as a Playwright was only beginning, and in fact a good deal of O'Neill's best work was still to come.

His private domestic life continued restless and unhappy. Within four years his father, mother, and brother had died. He brooded over his being the last of the O'Neills. In July, 1929, he and Agnes, his second wife, were divorced; two days later he married the famous beauty Carlotta Monterey, a former stage actress. She was to remain with him for the rest of his life, nursing him, during the final years, through the undiagnosable degenerative illness which took his life in 1953.

O'Neill's prolific output during the decade of the twenties includes, in addition to the works already mentioned, *The Hairy Ape*, *All God's Chillun Got Wings*, *Desire Under the Elms*, *Marco Millions*, *The Great God Brown*, *Lazarus Laughed*, *Strange Interlude*, *Dynamo*, and the first parts of *Mourning Becomes Electra*. O'Neill's restless spirit, always in rebellion against the limitations of established dramatic forms, was forever striving to break new ground. Strongly influenced by the experimental writing of his self-appointed model and mentor, August Strindberg, O'Neill struggled throughout his career with the problem of form, alternating between and often mixing naturalism, expressionism, and his own brand of dramatic poetry. The results were, predictably, uneven. *Lazarus Laughed*, for example, is a virtually unpredictable play, filled with heavy handed pseudo-poetry; its attempt to reintroduce the old Greek **convention** of masks into the American theater is generally regarded as an abysmal failure. *The Emperor Jones*, *The Hairy Ape*, and *Desire Under the Elms*, on the other hand, with their sharp, concise theatricality and their unique blending of **realism** and fantasy, exemplify in entirely different ways O'Neill's total mastery of dramatic form. *Strange Interlude* and *Mourning Becomes Electra* represent, among other things, not only their author's flirtation with the newly popular insights of a domesticated Freudianism, but also his attempts to do something "big," to break out of the confining straitjacket of conventional dramatic **realism**. A "big" play for O'Neill often meant merely a long play, a deliberate attempt to take his audiences into new areas of dramatic endurance.

The truth is, as O'Neill himself once wistfully admitted, that he often envied the novelist his domain. The actor's son who was himself so thoroughly a man of the theater frequently grew impatient with the problems and vicissitudes of production and deeply distrusted actors, producers, and directors. He once proclaimed, "I don't go to the theater because I can always do a better production in my mind than the one on the stage. I have a better time and I am not bothered by the audience. No one sneezes during the scenes that interest me." This distrust of the theater may account, at least partially, for the lengthy, elaborate stage directions he wrote into his plays.

The Last Plays: Between 1934, when *Days Without End* was produced in New York, and 1946, when *The Iceman Cometh* had its debut, no new O'Neill play appeared on the stage. After *Iceman* the next new play to be produced was the posthumously staged *Long Day's Journey into Night*, O'Neill's final cathartic attempt to come to terms with his father, mother, and brother, and, ultimately, with himself. Since his death in 1953 three other O'Neill plays have been produced: *A Touch of the Poet* (1957), *More Stately Mansions* (1962), and *Hughie* (1964). Like several other literary artists before him (Chaucer and Spenser, for example), O'Neill left unfinished a projected major work of huge design and scope. He failed to complete the vast dramatic saga he had planned, a work which, in eleven plays, would have traced the fortunes of one Irish American family through many generations and would have spanned American history, from colonial times to the present.

Regardless of history's final verdict on the work of Eugene O'Neill - and one suspects that it will be a mixed judgment - one fact remains indisputable. The man whose plays won him four Pulitzer Prizes and one Nobel Award, never gave up striving to translate into the idiom of the American stage his own deeply tragic sense of life. In response to a question from a newspaperman, O'Neill answered, in words which could very well be taken as his literary manifesto:

"I'll write about happiness if I ever happen to meet up with that luxury, and find it sufficiently dramatic and in harmony with any deep rhythm of life. But happiness is a word. What does it mean? Exaltation; an intensified feeling of the significant worth of man's being and becoming? Well, if it means that - and not a mere smirking contentment with one's lot - I know there is, more of it in one real tragedy than in all the happy-ending plays ever written. It's sheer present-day judgment to think of tragedy as unhappy. The Greeks and the Elizabethans knew better. They felt the tremendous lift to it. It roused them spiritually to a deeper understanding of life. Through it they found release from the petty considerations of everyday existence. They saw their lives ennobled by it. A work of art is always happy. All else is unhappy."

This is not the place, even if such a thing were possible, to attempt an exhaustive summary of O'Neill's life and work. We might rest content, for the moment, with the words spoken. To him on the occasion of his receiving an honorary doctorate from Yale University. The citation from Yale reads in part: "[Eugene O'Neill is] a creative contributor of new and moving forms to one of the oldest of the arts and is the first American playwright to receive both wide and serious recognition upon the stage of Europe."

Strange Interlude: O'Neill's career as a dramatist began, as we have seen, with the writing of one-act plays, a form that was relatively popular with the avant-garde writers of the day. It was not long, however, before he turned, not merely to the conventional, full-length play, but to the "big" play, or as it has been called, the "multi-play." *Marco Millions*, published in 1927, produced in 1928, and recently revived by the Lincoln Center Repertory Theater in its first season, was originally the first of the big plays. (Its present version represents O'Neill's condensation of two plays into one.) O'Neill, impatient with the severe limitations imposed on his grandiose ideas by the conventional demands of the dramatic form, frequently pushed beyond those limitations in his groping for the fullest possible treatment of his subject. He attempted to win for the playwright the spaciousness and artistic elbowroom enjoyed by the novelist. He was, furthermore, fully aware that people would come to know his plays as much by reading them as by seeing them staged. Many of his plays were published before they were produced, and he himself preferred reading plays to seeing them. It is possible that O'Neill's affection for the multi-play was buttressed by the example of Strindberg, who several times had tried his hand at the same kind of thing. It may be significant too that not long before the debut of *Strange Interlude* in 1928 the same Theater Guild which was to produce O'Neill's play had, in 1922, successfully staged Shaw's *Back to Methuselah*, a great, sprawling five-play cycle which took three successive evenings to run its course.

Strange Interlude, completed in 1926, published and produced in 1928, contains nine acts, spans approximately twenty-five years in the lives of its characters, and plays from 5:30 P. M. till shortly after 11:00 P. M., with an eighty-minute intermission for dinner between acts five and six. We know that as early as 1923 O'Neill was making notes for this huge work, and in 1925 he spoke of having completed a scenario for what he called "my woman play. "In August, 1925, he wrote to a friend complaining about his troubles with this work. "I did most of a second scene two separate times," he wrote, "and tore them up before I got started on the really right one.... There's going to be more work on [this play] than on any previous one - much more - with no end to the going over and over it, before I'll be willing to call it done." The work was finished by the following year, and two years later it was presented to the reading as well as to the theater-going public, with Lynn Fontanne in the lead role. Despite its length, *Strange Interlude* had the longest first run, a year and a half, of any O'Neill play. Two touring companies, one of them starring Judith Anderson, shortly thereafter took the play on the road and met with a like measure of success. In 1961 Jose Quintero revived the play off Broadway but this time the production, while provoking a good deal of interested response, was greeted with more restrained enthusiasm than in 1928.

Strange Interlude, with its powerful central character, Nina Leeds, is the result of, among other things, O'Neill's attempt to create the modern American version of Everywoman. In her is embodied the fullness of the dramatist's conception of the feminine principle. The play is also characterized by large doses of the Freudianism which was so popular among the intelligentsia during the twenties. The Freudian tags and clinical jargon, which would strike any sophisticated undergraduate today as somewhat old-fashioned, were, we must remember, new and exciting categories at the time of the play's composition. O'Neill's interest in psychiatry can probably be dated from his own brief fling at psychoanalysis in 1924. But concerning his use in *Strange Interlude* of explicitly psychiatric motivations for his characters' behavior, he declared, "I feel that although [it] is full of psychoanalytical ideas, still these same ideas are age-old to the artist and that any artist who was a good psychologist... could have written 'S. I.' without ever having heard of Freud, Jung, Adler, and Co...."

The other immediately noticeable feature about this work is its use of elaborate asides. In O'Neill's hands, however, the old theatrical convention becomes a major force for probing and revealing character. As he explained it, "Everything is a matter of **convention**. If we accept one, why not another, so long as it does what it's intended to do? My people speak aloud what they think and what the others aren't supposed to hear." The aside in this play has become the dramatic counterpart of what in many twentieth-century novels (such as those by Virginia Woolf and James Joyce) has been called the stream-of-consciousness technique or, more accurately, the interior monologue. Once again we find O'Neill attempting to annex for the stage one of the literary weapons of the novelist. In *Strange Interlude* the **convention** of allowing the audience to eavesdrop on the unspoken thoughts of the characters is intended not only to explore more deeply the psychic recesses of those characters, but also to intensify the dramatic conflict by presenting the clash between the hidden thought or emotion and its verbalized expression.

Strange Interlude, a work which has been vigorously attacked and equally vigorously defended, is a unique blend of unusual length, large chunks of half-digested Freudianism, and long, self-revealing asides. Whatever its merits - or lack of them - this play, like its creator, cannot be ignored.

CAST OF CHARACTERS

Charles Marsden, writer, old friend of Professor and Nina Leeds Professor Henry Leeds Nina Leeds, his daughter Edmund Darrell, a doctor, later Nina's lover Sam Evans, Nina's husband Mrs. Amos Evans, Sam's mother Gordon Evans, Nina's son Madeline Arnold, Gordon's fiancée

STRANGE INTERLUDE

CONCLUSION

O'NEILL AND AMERICAN LITERATURE

When Eugene O'Neill began to write, American drama was limited to insipid melodrama and trivial comedy. It had never been considered part of American literature, as such. More than any other playwright O'Neill helped to create a serious American drama. He did so by remaining uncompromisingly himself. His goal was not the creation of a serious American drama, but rather the full expression of the truth he believed he had in him. Indeed, he felt that America had failed. One of the central **themes** of his incomplete cycle of plays dealing with American history was the destruction of people through greed.

THE MEN O'NEILL ADMIRED

The men O'Neill admired did not possess great wealth or high position in society. He had learned in his seafaring days to admire simple men who responded directly to the challenge of a hostile world. And in spite of what he considered the hostility of the world, O'Neill obviously took great delight in an adventurous life lived close to nature. Like Paddy of *The Hairy Ape*, he longed for the days of sailing ships. He did not feel at home in the modern world. Whenever one of the down-and-out friends of his youth appealed to him for aid, he responded with immediate generosity, much to the dismay of his third wife who felt he had risen above their company.

THE PROBLEM OF MODERN MAN

O'Neill was an autobiographical writer. He said he had never written anything he had not experienced either directly or indirectly. He was far more interested in the relationship of individuals with the world than with each other. The chief problem of modern man, as he saw it, was the death of the old, orthodox conception of God and the inability of science and materialism to provide a new one for the religious instinct that yet survived. The sea of faith had retreated, leaving man high and dry.

O'NEILL'S ANSWER

O'Neill's answer to this problem is not a happy one. Man is alone in the universe and yet he must not knuckle under. Above all he must continue to follow his dream, whatever that may be. He must keep himself free from the corrupting power of wealth and position. Above all he must not sell out to the easy life, but continue to strive for the unknowable, no matter what the cost.

HIS DRAMATIC IMAGINATION

O'Neill had a comprehensive imagination and a broad experience of life. The sheer scope and power of his plays overwhelm the audience. Like Dreiser, he was deficient as a literary stylist. He was not, in fact, a literary writer, nor would he have wanted to be thought one. Although capable of writing eloquent prose, there is little poetry of language in his plays. However, intensity of emotion, breadth of scope and originality of plot more than make up for the lack of poetry. The chief defect of his plays is their length, and he cut them readily right up to the day of production. It is likely that future performances of his major plays will be freely cut by directors.

HIS INFLUENCE

It is hard to determine O'Neill's influence on contemporary American drama. He demonstrated that important **themes** could be handled on the stage and would be respected by American audiences. And yet it is difficult to find individual playwrights who have been influenced by him. In terms of his dramatic style he was far too original to be easily imitated, and he had an unusually creative mind that was continually searching for new techniques of expression. Certainly no twentieth century poet or novelist has experimented so broadly with his art. He was immensely prolific and constantly at work on some literary project Often ideas for new plays would come to him before he had finished the one he was working on. It is likely that future literary historians will see in O'Neill the father of serious dramatic literature in America. Before his plays there is very little worth discussing.

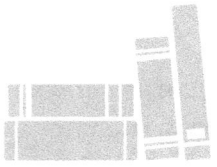

STRANGE INTERLUDE

CHARACTERS ANALYSES

Nina

A Case History? It is deceptively simple to dismiss Eugene O'Neill's penetrating study of a modern restless, love-hungry woman as nothing more than the case history of a neurotic female, driven by guilt and frustration to destroy herself and others. Aided and abetted by the heavy-handed psychologizing which tends to weigh down this play, many of O'Neill's critics have succumbed to the temptation to reduce the heroine of *Strange Interlude* to a few simplistic psychoanalytic categories. That O'Neill is interested in probing the psychic roots of Nina Leeds' behavior is, of course, obvious. It is not so obvious, however, that O'Neill's heroine can be facilely and neatly labeled and dismissed, any more than flesh and blood human beings can be. Knowing references to neurosis, fixations, pathogenic traumata, regressions, will simply not do if one wishes to come anywhere near exhausting the elusive and inexhaustible mysteriousness of this fascinating creature. The categories of modern psychoanalysis - which become mere cant phrases on the lips of the uninstructed - are undoubtedly of minimal utility in attempting to probe the rich complexities and tantalizing mystery of Nina Leeds. Such categories do not, however, end the discussion; they inaugurate it. To remain content with clumsily wielded labels borrowed from modern psychiatry is to succumb to a facile rationalism which does less than justice to the strange heroine of *Strange Interlude*. It is especially important in discussing Nina Leeds to make this point strongly and clearly, because the temptation to reduce her to a set of labels is enticingly present, planted by the playwright himself.

Illustrious Company: It can be claimed with some justification that Nina Leeds can take her place beside those other illustrious neurotic heroines of modern dramatic literature: Ibsen's Hedda Gabler, Strindberg's Miss Julie, and Tennessee Williams' Blanche Dubois in *A Streetcar Named Desire*. Like them she is psychically wounded, emotionally stunted; like them she is driven by a destructive force which ultimately turns in upon herself; and like them, finally, she has a meaning which transcends the merely psychological, a meaning which reaches out toward the domain of the symbolic in order to express its full significance.

Nina As Everywoman: It has become a **cliché** of contemporary O'Neill criticism to speak of Nina Leeds as a modern "Everywoman." The disturbing fact about many clichés, however, is that while they frequently contain a truth, or at least a partial truth, they just as frequently conceal beneath the dead language of the hackneyed formula as much truth as they reveal. Nina Leeds as Everywoman is undoubtedly a useful concept, but again, like the categories of psychology, it is not exhaustive of its subject. It is, after all, a critical construct, with all of the strengths and all of the limitations of any construct. First, the limitations.

The term Everywoman implies an allegorized abstraction, an intellectualized, inhuman stage character. The associations of the word with the fifteenth-century morality play Everyman are as inevitable as they are misleading. True, Nina Leeds fulfills all of the roles available to a woman in modern society. True, at one point especially - the end of Act Six - she takes on the stature of an outsized, **epic** figure, who at least for the moment is transfigured and stands before us as an earth goddess, as the embodiment of Woman. On the whole, however, she is a very particularized, carefully individuated woman - living in this house, wearing that dress, married to that man, adulterously loving this doctor, giving birth to this son, speaking and acting in a consistent, plausibly human fashion. To the extent that the term Everywoman might conceal such realities from us, then to that extent is it a limited, misleading word. It is perfectly true, of course, that the critic who first pinned this label on Nina, Edwin A. Engel (in his excellent study *The Haunted Heroes of Eugene O'Neill*) used it with delicacy and sophistication as a key by which to unlock some of the intricacies hidden in this fictional woman.

Nina As Rebel: While it is true that Nina remains a particularized woman who does, however, play a fascinating variety of roles, it is equally true that, paradoxically, she remains a pathetically unfulfilled human being who, at the play's end, can find no comfort but that of death. She is a victim of her own romantic rebellion against the human situation. Reaching out beyond herself, straining against the limitations of her humanity, she challenges as a woman-daughter-wife-lover-mother the supremacy of God the Father, who is indifferent to the world of his creation. Nina's rejection, on several levels, of the father figure unleashes, in a distorted, destructive fashion, the creative energy within her which drives her to challenge God the Father's supremacy over the universe. She becomes, to some extent, a symbol of the creative, feminine principle of fertility. She is, it might be said, the embodiment of Eros, that yearning, driving force which, as a result of its **metaphysical** quest for absolute fulfillment, Denis de Rougemont associates with death, in his brilliantly provocative but erratic study, *Love in the Western World*. Her revolt, her challenge, is doomed to failure, since she inhabits a world, a society, in which life, meaning, creativity can play no part. Her ultimate failure, then, is as much the result of the sickness of the human situation as it is the result of her internal psychic illness. It is this facet of Nina - Nina in metaphysical revolt against the conditions of existence - which lends to O'Neill's heroine a symbolic, larger-than-life dimension and which justifies the cautious use of the term Everywoman as an accurate description of her.

Nina's Dynamism: The most striking quality about Nina Leeds, aside from but obviously associated with her anxiety-riddled drive for power, is her dynamism. She is, between Acts One and Nine, a woman in the process of becoming. In her romantic search for an absolute fulfillment of her womanhood, she rejects in turn each feminine role which modern society makes available to its women, and she rejects these roles as static, limiting, encumbering. She announces her goal, without as yet realizing the full implications of what she is saying, in Act One: "I'm not myself yet. That's just it. Not all myself. But I've been becoming myself. And I must finish!" Nina's search for the absolute turns life into what Mario Praz calls the "romantic agony." Her revolt against time, history, humanity, her refusal to be satisfied with anything less than absolute happiness and peace can find fulfillment only in the final release which is death. Nina is a feminine version of Camus' rebel, a twentieth-century expression of the romantic lover whose search for the ecstasy of fulfillment is a metaphysical counterpart of Freud's death wish.

Interaction Of The **Metaphysical** And The Psychological: This larger significance of Nina Leeds is at least as important as her existence as an anguish-ridden modern woman neurotically destroyed by a repressive civilization and by an indifferent universe. These two facets of Nina Leeds - the **metaphysical** and the psychological - cannot, except for purposes of analysis, be isolated from each other. They reinforce one another and finally coalesce into the single fictional entity who is the heroine of the play. To take one obvious and central example of the interaction of the psychological and **metaphysical** in Nina's process of becoming, her rejection of God the Father, of the male principle in creation, is buttressed and to some extent produced by her rejection of her earthly father, Professor Leeds. In O'Neill's hands psychoanalytic theory, especially the Jungian variety, has become a tool for theological probing.

Edmund Darrell

A Key Male Figure: Probably the most important male figure in Nina Leeds' life - if it is possible to make such a distinction - is the attractive young doctor who enters the action as a scientist mildly interested in "her case," and who ends up fatally attracted to this fascinating woman. While it is certainly true that each of the men in Nina's life is important to her in different ways and at different times, these others function more or less as constants, as fixed points in the life of this restless woman. Gordon Shaw's ghost is a haunting presence throughout the entire action of the play, but he is a myth, a legend, and as such he has no more reality than the petrified reality possessed by any of the heroes of hagiography, whether secular or sacred. Charles Marsden, "dear old Charlie," is likewise always with us, living in the twilight world of suppressed love, waiting patiently on the sidelines for Nina to turn to him. Sam Evans is throughout the play essentially simple and trusting, although the mild arrogance which results from his financial success tends to reduce his simplicity to mere fatuousness. He remains, however, essentially unchanged. Gordon Evans, who enters late in the play's action, is a one-dimensional figure. A successful athlete, Gordon is confident that he will be an equally successful businessman.

Transformation: Ned Darrell, on the other hand, is another matter. His character, his values and attitudes undergo several radical changes in the course of the action, all directly resulting from his involvement with Nina Leeds. He is without a doubt the most dynamically drawn man in this work, which O'Neill once referred to as his "woman play." Disdainfully aloof when we first see him, he is surrounded by that aura of confidence which is the result of our society's deification of its medical men. The posture with which he meets life is that of the man in charge, the man who has the knowledge and the strength to control situations, and even people. (His first act onstage is, significantly, imperiously to order Sam Evans to run off and have a prescription filled for Nina.) This posture of the dominating male soon crumbles, however before the driving force of Nina's needs, instincts, and will power. He succumbs quickly and meekly to this single-minded woman. As Nina's lover, he becomes enthralled by her flesh, attempts to entice her away from her husband, and, failing this, falls into a bitter cynicism and dissipation which very nearly destroy him. He finally is able to free himself from the bondage of Nina's sexuality and pick up the scattered remains of his scientific career, but right down to the very last act Nina is still able to evoke some of the old desire in her ex-lover as she tries one last time to use this man in her desperate struggle for happiness.

As is befitting his role as Nina's lover, Darrell is a man with a magnetism, a dynamism of his own, though his strength is no match for Nina's. He changes, he evolves, he develops, to some extent he grows. One can hardly describe him as ennobled by his suffering, but at least he has fewer illusions about himself and his abilities than when we first met him. Significantly, he has shifted his attention from neurology to biology, a "cleaner" area of research, an area where one is not called upon or tempted to "meddle" in human lives.

The Failure Of Science: Through his characterization of Ned Darrell, O'Neill succeeds in tacitly and at times openly indicting modern science for its inability to supply a satisfactory meaning to life's mysteries. The playwright, in a passage quoted earlier, spoke bluntly about the failure of science and materialism "to give any satisfying new God for the surviving primitive religious instinct to find a meaning for life in." Darrell is not only the doctor, the healer, who ironically winds up healing no one, including himself. He also symbolizes, as a scientist, the dominant, godlike figure of our technological culture. In the popular imagination he is the master, the one supposedly in possession of the tribal magic which unlocks the secret of the universe. His science, however, proves inadequate as a response to the mystery, the cruelty, the beauty, the passions, the volatility of human existence. As a healer he prescribes remedies which prove ineffectual; as the prophet of a new Weltanschauung, or world view, he is irrelevant. He is forced at the end to retreat before the unpredictabilities, the contingencies, the irrationalities of existence, and his return to scientific research at a symbolically remote biology station is in fact a surrender, a withdrawal from living. Darrell's failure must not be seen simply as the playwright's polemical urge to discredit science. It is rather the result of O'Neill's distrust of the mystique of science, and the myth of the scientist as the omniscient seer is nowhere more clearly exposed than in the failures of Doctor Edmund Darrell.

Weak Characterization? One generally astute critic of O'Neill's works, Edwin A. Engels, has argued that "of Nina's four men, Darrell is the least probable figure." Engels goes on to account for what he regards as a weak characterization by suggesting that "O'Neill's scorn for the scientist caused him to overcompensate when he portrayed Nina's lover." It is difficult to accept such an interpretation, since Darrell is neither caricatured as a villain nor is he idealized as a swashbuckling, romantic hero. His love affair with Nina is not, as Engels puts it, "sentimental." The afternoons of erotic ecstasy are quickly followed by disillusion and resentment. The bitterness and hollowness which characterize Darrell in the last acts of the play have emerged plausibly and intelligibly from the **episodes** depicting his failure to win and hold Nina permanently and exclusively as his own, and from his refusal to claim his son as his own. Engels criticizes O'Neill for having offered "no sufficient cause for Nina's increasingly sad condition nor for Darrell's protracted suffering," and he comments in another place, "That love is superseded, after eleven years, by faded passion should have come as little surprise to a man trained in biology." Such a view fails to take into account the crucially important distinction between the cerebral knowledge of a truth and the visceral living of that truth. Darrell's bitterly won experiential awareness of what he previously knew only as a scientifically demonstrable datum is actually on a different level of human knowledge. It is precisely this distance between the cerebral and the visceral which ironically defines Darrell's existence in this play. This self-confident man of intellect is brought down through his hybris, his intellectual pride, and he is forced to relearn and repossess through the sufferings of lived experience those textbook truths which he had known only in a partial, sterile way.

Charles Marsden

A Static Character: Of the major characters in the play, Charles Marsden is probably the most wooden. The leitmotifs with which we associate this man are introduced in the opening moments of the play and remain as constants through the entire action: an Oedipal attachment to his mother, a loathing for sex, an attachment to Nina compounded of paternal solicitude and suppressed sexual desire. Marsden is predictable and static, and as such his characterization is weak and shallow, displaying none of the subtleties and varieties we expect from a fully drawn, complex creation. Dramatic economy as well as Marsden's inherent passivity combine to make this genteel novelist an uninteresting, superficially conceived figure. One suspects too that O'Neill may have been indulging in some ax-grinding when he created Marsden, for while it is true that Darrell and Evans are depicted as symbolic representatives of two sets of values of which the dramatist disapproves, we do not readily detect the polemical tone in O'Neill's condemnation of what they stand for. In the character of Marsden, on the other hand, one notices an extra bite, an edge of sharpness in the dramatist's portrayal of the man who dabbles in literary art. As a dedicated literary artist himself, O'Neill might understandably have found it difficult to suppress his resentment of the pseudo-artist. The result, however, borders on caricature.

Freudian Categories: The dramatist's attempts to add complexity to this character by contrasting the fastidious decorum of his surface life with the repressed energies and turbulence of his inner life do not really succeed. The rather simplistic use of Freudian categories in establishing Marsden's character accomplish little in the way of raising him to the level of the believably human. His mother fixation is too patently clear to be psychologically convincing. His arrested sexual development as a result of his one and only sexual experience - with a prostitute when he was sixteen - is too stridently insisted upon by the playwright, is too clearly present to Marsden's consciousness to be psychiatrically valid. These two psychic notes are loudly and forcefully struck in most of his interior monologues. One tends to get bored with O'Neill's facile definitions of Charles Marsden. Without sacrificing artistic proportion, the dramatist could have succinctly developed some of the subtleties and complexities which are present in every human being, fictional or actual, and which are certainly present potentially in a cultivated New England novelist, who knowingly turns his back on life and who is caught between the demands of a repressive civilization and his own primitive yearnings and instincts as a man. Instead of probing and illuminating this agonizing conflict, O'Neill chose to remain satisfied with the **clichés** of an oversimplified Freudianism. O'Neill's failure, generally speaking, with the character of Charles Marsden, can be chalked up as a casualty of his sophomoric dabbling in the murky waters of psychoanalysis.

A Death Figure: Marsden, as the sexually repressed, mother-dominated eunuch, is also the father figure, and since the father (both God and Professor Leeds) is associated with death in this play, then quite naturally and easily Marsden, who in the later acts of the play is always in mourning and always reminding us of death, becomes a death symbol. His association with spiritual and biological death is merely another dimension of the death of sexuality and artistry in his own life. At the end of the interlude of Nina's unsuccessful struggle for happiness, she retrogressively returns, as we have seen, to Charles Marsden: to her father, to a life which no longer includes sex - in a word, to death. Marsden in the last act has become almost pure symbol. Dressed in black, he interrupts the passionate embrace ("biological preparations" he sneeringly thinks to himself) of Gordon and Madeline. He is carrying a pair of shears (reminiscent of the death-dealing sister in the trio of the Fates) and a bunch of freshly cut and therefore dying roses. The historically rich symbolism of the rose, its association with the brevity of life and love, are obvious. It is a short distance from static, shallow characterization to the status of symbol, and Charles Marsden has covered the distance without difficulty, since in neither one of these roles does anything approaching a flesh and blood reality ever actually intrude.

Sam Evans

Sam Evans, the arrested adolescent of the play's early acts, seems suddenly to blossom and mature as the play develops, largely as a result of his marriage and the birth of a son who is not, ironically, his own. The birth of young Gordon imparts an inner self-assurance to the young man who up until that time was characterized by diffidence, trusting simplicity, weakness and bumbling incompetence. His transformation into the self-confident, almost brash, man of business borders on the miraculous. His achievement may be regarded as a tacit indictment of the financial community and of America's shallow cult of success. At the peak of his career he still worships the memory of his dead classmate, Gordon Shaw, who was the handsome, virile, successful, all-around, all-American boy. Evans is the guardian of the Gordon myth, passing on to young Gordon tales of the dead hero's athletic feats and instilling in the young man the puerile view which sees collegiate athletic prowess as life's greatest good. Sam Evans is the embodiment of O'Neill's vision of the business community's values: facile congeniality, intellectual immaturity, shallow optimism, philistinism.

Art Triumphs Over Propaganda: Probably the most remarkable fact to be noted about O'Neill's characterization of Evans is that the playwright allowed him to come through as a relatively attractive person. One recalls that *Strange Interlude* is the product of an era when it was intellectually fashionable to join H. L. Mencken in sneering at the "booboisie," an era presided over by a mediocre president whose most memorable pronouncement was, "The business of America is business." It was an age when the deep rift between the business and artistic communities was a markedly pronounced fact of American life. Babbitt, the hero of Sinclair Lewis's novel of the same name published in 1922, became the symbol of all that was vulgar and boorish in an American society dominated by the superficial values of the progress myth. O'Neill, whose artistic roots were deeply imbedded in Greenwich Village bohemianism, was also nourished by the socialism and political anarchy which were parts of the literary landscape of the twenties. In view of the intellectual matrix out of which *Strange Interlude* emerged, it is noteworthy that O'Neill was able to exercise enough restraint in creating Sam Evans to escape the temptation to turn him into a satirical caricature. O'Neill, of course, never one to succumb to intellectual or artistic fads, was always his own man, and his artistic integrity generally preserved him from the lures of propaganda. While it is true that prior to the composition of *Strange Interlude* O'Neill had pessimistically announced his abandonment of political and social causes, he had not given up the values which had initially led to his distrust of the vulgar materialism of American business.

In pointing out that in his conception of Sam Evans' character O'Neill has on the whole avoided the ideological shrillness of the doctrinaire left, we must be careful not to overstate the case. Evans is by no means a hero in O'Neill's eyes, and we are never allowed to ignore the sterility and fatuousness of his existence.

Despite Evans' contentment, O'Neill does not allow his audience to forget that his success, as a businessman, as a husband, as a father, is shaky and hollow. It remains true, however, that Eugene O'Neill, the artist, was much more interested in the personal relationships between Evans and the other characters than he was in the propaganda potentialities of this naive, good-natured cipher.

Professor Leeds

Professor Leeds, Nina's father, who dies between Acts One and Two, is from one point of view not only a minor character but an insignificant one. One might speculate as to why O'Neill chose to include him at all, since the dramatist could have begun his play later, at the point where Leeds has died and Nina has returned home for the funeral. It is clear, however, that what the playwright has lost in dramatic economy he has gained in theatrical immediacy and artistic symmetry. In the first place, it is obviously more effective to present the conflict between Nina and her father rather than report it in retrospect. Secondly, if the play's action is to consist of Nina's cyclic journey, beginning with her abandonment of the father and concluding in a return to the father, then the play achieves a greater artistic balance by paralleling Act One with Act Nine, Professor Leeds with Charles Marsden.

Contrast To Nina: Leeds is a sketchily developed character. His principal function in the play is to trigger Nina's restless wanderings by preventing her marriage to Gordon, and also to act as a foil to his neurotically energetic daughter. He is dull, prim, pompously pedantic in contrast to Nina, who, throughout much of the action, is vibrantly alive. His bookish immersion in classical literature has become an escape, a withdrawal from the modern world. He has - like Marsden but on his own terms - substituted the "dead" languages and cultures of Greece and Rome for the complex, unpleasant realities of daily living. Like Marsden too, his person and his surroundings emanate the presence of death, and this identification of the father with death becomes, as we have seen, an important thematic element in the play. Act One closes with his presentiments of his own imminent death, and as the curtain falls he reads in Latin a passage dealing with isolation and death.

Mrs. Evans

Mrs. Evans, Sam's mother, appears only in Act Three, where her primary, in fact her only, role is to reveal to Nina the secret of the insanity in the Evans family. The device of revealing a dark secret out of the past, a commonplace of nineteenth and early twentieth-century realistic drama, is handled by O'Neill in a manner which skillfully makes of the revelation a vital piece of dramatic action. To further this end, O'Neill made of Mrs. Evans something more than a neutral, theatrically insignificant messenger. She has, for her short time on the stage, distinguishing characteristics and a life of her own. She has become a slave to the cause of salvaging happiness for others, especially for her son, out of the darkness and misery which surround her. Her dedication to preserving her husband's sanity proved futile. She is now equally dedicated to nursing her husband's sister, who lives in solitude and mental blankness on the top floor of the house. Her son knows nothing of the hereditary insanity afflicting his family, and Mrs. Evans is determined to keep the knowledge from him as her sole remaining duty in life. Such a bleak existence has, of course, embittered this woman. She grimly reveals to Nina her loss of faith: "And I don't believe in Him, neither, not anymore. I used to be a great one for worrying about what's God and what's devil, but I got richly over it living here with poor folks that was being punished for no sins of their own, and me being punished with them for no sin but loving much." Her interior monologue discloses, furthermore, the ambivalence of her motives in breaking the dreadful news to Nina: "I know what she's doing now...just what I did trying not to believe... But I'll make her!... she's got to suffer, too! ...I been too lonely!..."

Mrs. Evans, then, although a decidedly secondary character in the play, has been drawn with a skill and economy which makes her brief appearance a moving and believable one.

GORDON EVANS

Gordon Evans, the product of the Nina-Darrell love affair which tried to masquerade as a scientific experiment, is a late entry, not appearing until Act Seven, when we first encounter him on his eleventh birthday. His very presence before the audience is a harsh reminder of the passage of time. As the physical embodiment of the passionate relationship between his mother and Darrell, a relationship which has now faded into bitterness, Gordon plays a pivotal role in the complicated web of relationships which Nina has spun about herself. He loves and admires Sam, whom he regards as his real father; is affectionate toward Uncle Charlie Marsden; but he is resentful and distrustful toward Darrell, whom he looks upon as an intruder. His animosity toward the scientist, who periodically drops into their lives from his remote research station, is confirmed and deepened when he sees Nina and Darrell embracing and kissing during a rare interlude of affection in their generally corroded relationship. As the symbolic reincarnation of the dead hero who was his mother's fiancé, young Gordon is jealous of Darrell, his rival for Nina's affections. In a variation on the

Oedipus **theme**, the son competes with the father for the love of the mother. Toward the end of Act Seven we see Gordon eagerly devouring Sam's stories about the heroic accomplishments of his dead namesake, the Gordon who, though dead, has remained the rival of all of Nina's men for her love.

Gordon never appears in Act Eight, but his presence permeates the stage. Everyone has gathered on the Evans motor launch to observe his crew's victory in the final varsity regatta of his collegiate career. The ending of the race, which takes place offstage and is reported by the spectators on the launch, sees Gordon Evans slumped over in a dead faint, just as Gordon Shaw had done many years before in his last varsity race. This is only one among many in the cycle of events which repeat themselves in the final acts of the play.

Gordon in Act Nine, accompanied by his fiancée, Madeline Arnold - who is reminiscent of Nina at that age - is mourning the death of Sam and is still deeply hostile toward Ned Darrell. After his explosive scene with the man who is, still unknown to him, his real father, he takes his leave and flies off into a future which will include a wedding, a honeymoon in Europe, and a successful business career. His life will be the kind of which Sam Evans would have heartily approved. Just as the play opened with the memory of Gordon Shaw's death in a flaming airplane, so does it close with the new Gordon flying away triumphantly, escaping the world of darkness and despair which envelops those who remain.

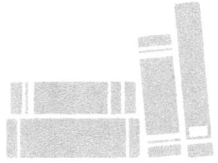

STRANGE INTERLUDE

STRUCTURAL ANALYSIS

CIVILIZATION: HEALER OR DESTROYER?

Acts One and Two take place in Professor Leeds' library-study, where we meet first the Professor, then his novelist friend just returned from Europe, Charles Marsden, and finally the heroine, Nina Leeds. O'Neill seems to be suggesting through his stage setting a visual counterpart of the action-of his play - the scene for Acts One and Two, in its rigid, antiseptic orderliness, by implication stands for the repressive emotional atmosphere which is at the root of Nina's problems. If, as O'Neill seems to be saying, Professor Leeds has immersed himself in a study of the past, and Marsden has retreated into the writing of lifeless novels, and Nina is about to flee her home in a search for emotional peace, then the audience is led to conclude that the first three characters we encounter are driven in their several ways by a need to escape the realities of the present and the ghosts of the past.

In each case it would seem that it is the repressive dimension of civilization which has turned these three figures into haunted, fearful people with the odor of death and destruction about them.

Leeds, the professor of classics; Marsden, the sexually timid, mother-dominated writer of genteel novels; Nina, the guilt-haunted, neurotic young woman whose life has been shattered by the death of her fiancé in the war-all of these people, O'Neill implies, are victims of a civilizing process which has left little or no room for the healthy flourishing of the emotional life. They are, it might be said, over-civilized. This point becomes even clearer when we learn that Nina's guilt stems directly from the fact that she did not marry Gordon Shaw before he left for the war; this guilt, we learn, has been deepened by Nina's refusal to give herself sexually to Gordon. The prim, proper, fastidious Professor Leeds blocked the marriage and helped to instill. In his daughter those inhibitions which prevented her from giving herself to the man she loved. When Nina announces her intention to devote her life to nursing wounded war veterans, we can see both in her announcement and in her father's and Marsden's horrified reaction, not only the results of the past, but the seeds of conflict for the future.

BRIEF CHARACTER ANALYSIS

1. Charles Marsden reveals himself in this act as a person whose emotional life is severely inhibited, particularly in his attitudes toward sex. He is closely identified with Professor Leeds, as both an ex-student and as a friend. He is, without daring to admit it to himself, in love with Nina, but he has sublimated whatever sexuality exists in the attraction into a paternal concern to protect her. This foreshadows the relationship which ultimately develops in the last act of the play when Nina agrees to marry this older man who has become a sexually neutral, second father to her.

2. Professor Leeds appears only in this act of the play, dying as he does before the opening of Act Two. He is a fastidious widower who pursues the safe life of classical scholarship and who wants the warmth and comfort of spending the rest of his life having his daughter wait on him. This is the real reason, as he admits under Nina's sharp questioning, why he prevented her marriage to Gordon. When she announces her intention of leaving him, there is nothing left for him to do but look forward to his impending death.

3. Nina is a distraught, haunted figure throughout this act. Her sense of loss as a result of Gordon's death is aggravated by feelings of guilt over her refusal to give herself to Gordon before his departure. It is these feelings which prompt her decision to leave home to work in a hospital for wounded soldiers-an attempt at expiation.

Comment

Although O'Neill in this play adapted certain techniques found only in the novel, and despite the fact that a great many people read this play the way they would a novel, it becomes all the more important to stress at the outset that *Strange Interlude* is a dramatic work of art and, like any play, it must be read as such. This means, among other things, that the action must constantly be visualized, must be staged by the inner eye and ear of the reader A play's action must be seen, at least in the imagination, its dialogue heard, its characters positioned or "blocked," its sets created and played in. To ignore this dimension of a drama is to remove oneself as a reader even further from the only way in which a play may be truly experienced, that is, in its existence on a stage.

O'Neill's elaborate comments and stage directions aid the reader immeasurably in re-creating this play as it might be produced in a theater. From the moment the curtain rises on *Strange Interlude*, even before anyone appears on the stage, the stage set should begin, in its own way, to communicate the emotions, ideas, and values which make up the meaning and texture of the play. The curtain rises, it will be recalled, on a room which is neat, orderly, regimented. Lined with books - editions of the classics - it is Professor Leeds' library, his haven, his retreat from the messy job of living. "It is a small room with a low ceiling," the playwright tells us, suggesting through the physical setting, through the visual impact of the stage props, something of the suffocating, anti-life atmosphere in which his characters have been living. When Charles Marsden enters this room alone, virtually the first words out of his mouth are, "Sanctum Sanctorum," the holy of holies. The dramatic **irony** is immense, for this room, we discover as the action unfolds, is a **metaphor** for the antiseptic, life-denying hell in which Professor Leeds and his daughter have been trying to exist. This library is a kind of clean, well-lighted tomb, and the motif of death slinks in and out of the words and hidden thoughts of the three characters who appear in this act. Charles Marsden recalls, in a passage strongly marked by echoes from the dramatist's own life: "Father...how dim his face has grown! ...he wanted to speak to me just before he died... the hospital...smell of iodoform in the cool halls...hot summer... I bent down...his voice had withdrawn so far away... I couldn't understand him...what son can ever understand? ...always too near, too soon, too distant or too late! ..."It is less important, as far as the play's artistry is concerned, that these lines closely parallel O'Neill's own experience at his father's deathbed, than that they obliquely foreshadow the chasm that exists between parent and child in this play and also dimly prepare for the death of the father, Professor Leeds. Nina, in her turn, is also obsessed with death. She thinks and talks throughout this act almost solely about her dead fiancé. And finally the Professor, left alone onstage at the end of the act, vividly foresees his own death in the not too distant future: "Then good-bye...a kiss... nothing more ever to say to each other...and I'll die in here some day...alone...gasp, cry out for help...the president will speak at the funeral... Nina will be here again... Nina in black...too late! ..." It is no exaggeration to say that death hovers over this act-and over the entire play-from beginning to end.

Exposition: One of the most important tasks facing the dramatist, particularly in the opening scenes of a play, is **exposition**. This involves, to put it simply, imparting to the audience, quickly and economically, enough information about the characters' past to make their present conversation and actions intelligible. We want to know the answers to such questions as: who is this man? what is he doing here? where has he come from? what does he do for a living? what is his relationship with and attitude toward this older man who has just entered the room? who is this Gordon whom everybody keeps referring to? how did he die? what do these two men feel toward the dead Gordon? toward the beautiful young girl who has just entered? what are her feelings toward the two men in the room? toward Gordon? toward herself? Such questions as these, and a host of others, are raised, consciously or unconsciously by the appearance of characters on a stage, talking and relating to each other. The **exposition**, accomplished through the characters' words, should provide the answers. Well-written dialogue, such as that found in Ibsen's plays, for example, reveals action in the present, exposes enough of the past to make that present action meaningful, and prepares for future developments and entanglements.

In *Strange Interlude* O'Neill accomplishes the **exposition** largely through the soliloquies and the unspoken thoughts of the characters, thoughts which the audience is privileged to listen in on. Charles Marsden, for instance, in his opening soliloquy tells us enough about himself, Professor Leeds, and Nina to allow us to understand the ensuing dialogue. Leeds, in his turn, through his conversation with Charles and through his asides, tells us a great deal about his daughter, both past and present, so that when Nina Leeds does make her carefully prepared entrance, we already possess enough information about her and the two men to make their dialogue intelligible. The **convention** of the soliloquy and the aside, which some have found clumsily handled, does, in any case, allow the dramatist to do the job of exposition relatively smoothly and quickly.

How To Stage The Asides: The question of how to present these asides and soliloquies, how to enable the audience to distinguish them from the regular spoken dialogue, posed a serious technical problem for the play's first director, Philip Moeller. Discarding several ideas-such as changes in lighting, two kinds of voices for the two levels of dialogue, special playing areas onstage for the delivery of the asides - Mr. Moeller finally decided upon a technique which he referred to as arrested motion. This involved the complete cessation of all physical movement, the, "freezing," of the other characters in position while any one character was delivering his "unspoken" thoughts. The device proved a successful means of communicating O'Neill's intentions to the audiences which attended the original 1928 production.

Danger Of Innovations: These technical experiments, however, are meaningful only insofar as they aid in involving the spectators in the emotional experiences and conflicts of the people on the stage. The danger is always present that theatrical innovations may tend to attract undue attention to themselves because of their novelty and reduce themselves to the level of mere "gimmicks," organically separated from the play they are supposed to serve. Any production of *Strange Interlude* must, if it is to achieve any degree of success, cope with this problem.

Repressed Emotion: The emotional conflicts in this play, as they begin to take shape in the first act, stem largely if not exclusively, from thwarted or repressed sexual expression. (This strong emphasis upon sex resulted in the play's being banned in Boston.) The stifled sexual dynamism of the play's central character, Nina Leeds, finds a variety of outlets as a result of her denial of her sexual love to the man whom she loved and who is now gone forever. As she exclaims to her father in an outburst which is the high point of emotional intensity in the first act: "But Gordon never possessed me! I'm Gordon's silly virgin! And Gordon is muddy ashes! And I've lost my happiness forever! All that last night I knew he wanted me. I knew it was only the honorable code-bound Gordon, who kept commanding from his brain, no, you mustn't, you must respect her, you must wait till you have a marriage license!" It is this sense of loss and its accompanying sense of guilt which impels her to play the variety of "woman" roles we see her in throughout the remaining eight acts of the play. It might be objected that the motivation of the characters' behavior is too explicitly clear to the characters themselves. The complex, murky depths which underlie human actions are rarely if ever seen with such simplicity and clarity as they are in this play.

Nina's Strong Entrance: Nina's first appearance on stage provides a powerful dramatic contrast to the two relatively lifeless, sexually neutral characters: the somewhat effeminate, mother-dominated Marsden, and the prim, fussy classics professor, She is a striking physical presence, particularly when seen against the foil of her father's library, that room in which the dead past has been enshrined. Her very first words, furthermore, reveal her as a creature of will: "I have made up my mind, Father." Her whole entrance scene, with its strong visual impact and its pregnantly significant opening line, is a perfect example of the soundness of O'Neill's dramatic instincts.

Lines Of Conflict Established: The potential lines of conflict, then, or at least some of them, are firmly established by the time the curtain falls on Act One. The conflict is, in each case, the result of the characters' war with themselves as well as with each other. It was this internal, psychological conflict which led O'Neill to reach out for new means of laying bare the inner, tormented psychic states of his characters.

DEATH AND ITS AFTERMATH

One watches the curtain falling at the end of Act One with the sense of death so palpable that it can almost be felt. Not only does the action take place in what might be described as a cultural mausoleum or tomb; not only does the presence of the dead flyer hover over the whole act; not only does Charles Marsden reveal his revulsion for the life-giving implicit in human sexuality; but Professor Leeds, as the curtain falls, is looking forward to his imminent death. As the curtain rises on Act Two, we find that Leeds has indeed died and Nina has just returned home for the funeral. The gloomy Marsden is there to greet her, and when we encounter in this act the two newcomers, Dr. Edmund Darrell and Sam Evans, we sense that the relentless force of death may be due for at least a temporary check. O'Neill seems to want his audience to look upon these two men as counterpoints to Charles Marsden and the two dead men, Gordon Shaw and Professor Leeds. When Darrell, a neurologist at the hospital where Nina had been working, informs Marsden that she has been sexually promiscuous with the wounded soldiers, Marsden arranges to marry Nina off to Evans. By the end of Act Two, new characters have been introduced, new relationships established and new lines of conflict set in motion.

Nina enters, discusses her inability to feel anything and her discovery of "the lies in the sounds called words." She tells Marsden, the writer, that with him "the lies have become the only truthful things." She also reveals her futile attempts to pray to "the modern science God" and concludes that "I couldn't believe in Him and I wouldn't if I could! I'd rather imitate his indifference and prove I had that one trait at least in common." Darrell leaves, Nina talks more about God and what He ought to be-a woman-and then tells Marsden about her need to be punished. At this point she reveals her sexual promiscuity with the hospital patients. Marsden is revolted, urges her to marry Evans, and she passively, pliably, agrees. She falls asleep, "like a little girl," and Marsden picks her up to carry her to her room. As he is leaving, Evans returns, is told by Marsden that he has reason to hope concerning his love for Nina, and is left alone onstage. Evans exclaims, "Good egg! Good old Charlie!" As the curtain falls, Marsden's bitter laugh is heard offstage.

BRIEF CHARACTER ANALYSIS

1. Charles Marsden is, on the whole, a static character throughout the nine acts of the play. This is dramatically appropriate since he is a sterile, uncreative person, one who is incapable of love, is afraid of sex and is, ultimately, the anti-life figure in the play. He remains Nina's constant lover, the fixed point in her agonized wanderings through life. He is confident that eventually she will turn to him, and he is right. In the last act she does turn to "dear old Charlie," when she is ready to give

up the struggle, when she is ready, as she puts it, to "rot in peace."

In Act Two Marsden in his soliloquy once again discloses the terror that sexual attraction holds for him and also tells of his weak, unnatural dependence on his aged, ailing mother. He is hopeful that Nina, returning home for her father's funeral, will throw herself into his arms and find strength and consolation in his presence. He is jealously distrustful of Darrell, whom we first encounter in this act, a young neurologist interested in Nina's "case." Marsden is patronizingly contemptuous toward Sam Evans, a callow youth who had known and hero-worshipped the dead Gordon Shaw. Marsden's unwillingness and inability to face reality are revealed in his reaction to Darrell's blunt disclosure concerning Nina's loose sexual behavior.'

2. Ned Darrell is masterful, dominant, knowledgeable, especially in contrast to the weak Marsden and the immature, arrested adolescent, Sam Evans. Doctor Darrell is clearly in charge of the situation, authoritatively disposing of people and their problems.

3. Evans, as already indicated, is an obsequious, awe-struck young bumpkin from the farm. He idolizes Nina, just as-he worships the memory of Gordon Shaw, who succeeded in everything he tried his hand at. Sam, by contrast, feels himself to be a failure at everything he attempts.

4. Nina Leeds is emotionally hollow, incapable of feeling anything over her father's death. Her attempts to quiet her inner turbulence by entering into a series of love

affairs at the hospital have only produced a state of near emotional paralysis. Her first attempts to find love and to quiet her anxiety have obviously failed. She is now about to embark on a series of further attempts.

Comment

Centrality Of Death: Just as Act One began with the memory of one death and with the premonition of another, so does Act Two begin with the fact of death. As the action begins, we learn that Professor Leeds has just died and that his daughter, who has been living a death-in-life existence, is about to return home for the funeral. As we shall see, another death, that of Nina's unborn child, is prepared for in Act Three and takes place between Acts Three and Four, and other deaths occur as the action develops. This concern with death is not merely an artificial, melodramatic attempt to heighten the sense of tragedy. Death is, after all, the ultimate, unavoidable fact of every human existence, and its centrality in *Strange Interlude*, especially in the early acts, quite naturally and organically provides O'Neill with the opportunity to probe the meaning of life and death and to raise the kind of large questions in which he was always interested. Nina Leeds, who is deeply affected and eventually transformed and redirected by the deaths which touch her so intimately-fiancé, father, unborn child-describes the human situation as "our trifling misery of death-born-of birth." Death in this play is a means by which the dramatist challenges, threatens and develops the humanity of his central character.

Return Of An Absent Character: This act is marked by another device also utilized in Act One, the return of someone who has been absent for a time, in this case, Nina. Return or reunion after absence has frequently been used by dramatists (Ibsen and Chekhov, for example) as a means of accomplishing several goals. For one thing, it makes **exposition** more natural, more plausible, since people who have been apart will, quite automatically, inform one another about events and changes that have occurred during the period of separation. For another thing, reunion often allows a more dramatic confrontation between people, for inevitably they have changed, have had new experiences, have possibly even developed new attitudes and values, Any such changes are etched more sharply, more dramatically, in the consciousness of people who have been apart. Both goals-ease of exposition and heightening of dramatic confrontation-are served by the reunion device in this and in the other acts in which the playwright makes use of it.

Grouping Of Characters: As is true of any play, *Strange Interlude* is, in its own way, essentially concerned with the dynamism of shifting human relationships and the joys, sorrows, and conflicts generated by those relationships. It might prove instructive to examine briefly the means the playwright employs to reveal his characters in abrasive contact with one another. On the assumption that a fuller grasp of the techniques and structure of a work of art will enhance our enjoyment of it, we might, somewhat schematically, trace the manner in which the dramatist groups and regroups his characters in this act. It is this arranging and rearranging of the characters which, skillfully done, develops action and unfolds complexity of character. Here is how O'Neill groups his people in this second act:

Marsden Marsden-Nina (briefly). Nina exits. Marsden-Evans Marsden-Evans-Darrell. Evans exits. Marsden-Darrell Marsden-Darrell-Nina. Darrell exits. Marsden-Nina Marsden-Nina-Evans. Marsden exits, carrying the sleeping Nina. Evans.

It will be seen at a glance that Marsden is onstage for virtually the entire second act, until the final few seconds when he is replaced by Evans. As Nina's new father figure, he is, relatively speaking, the central character in her life at this stage of her development. His yielding of the stage to Evans as the curtain falls (accompanied by Marsden's bitter offstage laughter) is a visual statement of his replacement by the younger Evans in the next stage of Nina's development. A survey of the combinations of characters listed above discloses, furthermore, that Nina makes her full entrance into the action only after the act is more than half finished, Even when physically absent from our sight, however, she still is present through her domination of the thoughts, actions, memories, and desires of every character onstage. Once again, as in Act One, the dramatist takes great pains to prepare the situation for his central character before he brings her onstage. In this way, by carefully preparing and building the emotional context, the playwright is able to achieve the maximum illumination and dramatic tension from the scenes involving his heroine. Each of the character combinations reveals, in a different way, a new facet of each of the characters, a new dimension of the developing action.

Offspring: In this act we hear the first mention of children - for Nina. She is not yet married, of course, but despite-or perhaps because of - the presence of death in the house she and the others look forward to her bearing offspring. For Dr. Darrell, the neurologist who talks and acts like a Freudian analyst, having children would provide Nina with "normal outlets for her craving for sacrifice." The man chosen to be her mate, Sam Evans, seems wholesome and healthy, and that he and his family are farmers, well-off fruit growers, serves further to associate this clean-cut young man with life and fertility. The choice of Evans is cruelly ironic, for, as it turns out, he is afflicted with hereditary insanity, the discovery of which leads to tragic entanglements for Nina.

Marsden As Father Figure: It has already been remarked that from the opening of the play Charles Marsden tends to assume, in his own mind as well as in Nina's, the role of a father figure toward her. This role emerges even more strongly and clearly as Act Two draws to a close. "You sound so like Father, Charlie," she says to him at one point. Nina's biological father is dead, and so is her theological father, God. Her need for a father takes her inevitably into the ambivalent, paternal arms of Marsden, who becomes, in addition to a God-father substitute, a father confessor, a kind of symbolic priest to whom she confesses her misdeeds and from whom she asks punishment, in a scene strongly reminiscent of a sacramental-confessional scene. After confessing to Marsden and receiving a secularized version of absolution, she says to him, "Thank you, Father. You've been so kind. You've let me off too easily. I don't feel as if you'd punished me hardly at all. But I'll never, never do it again, I promise - never, never!" Marsden's three surrogate roles - God, father, priest-confessor - clearly coalesce in Nina's mind here.

Rejection Of God: There is a good deal of talk about God throughout Act Two, most of it coming from the empty, embittered Nina. Marsden first introduces the specifically theological note when he exclaims in his opening soliloquy, "Everything in life is so contemptuously accidental! ...God's sneer at our self-importance!" Nina, however, makes the major theological pronouncements, and during several of them the spectator or reader gets the uneasy feeling that she is dangerously close to being the dramatist's puppet or mouthpiece. The voice may be Nina's, but the words and tonal urgency in such speeches as the following seem more O'Neill's than hers: "I wanted to believe in any God at any price-a heap of stones, a mud image, a drawing on a wall, a bird, a fish, a snake, a baboon-or even a good man preaching the simple platitudes of truth, those Gospel words we love the sound of but whose meaning we pass on to spooks to live by!" And she continues a few moments later, "The mistake began when God was created in a male image. Of course, women would see Him that way, but men should have been gentlemen enough, remembering their mothers, to make God a woman! But the God of Gods - the Boss - has always been a man. That makes life so perverted, and death so unnatural. We should have imagined life as created in the birth-pain of God the Mother. Then we would understand why we, Her children, have inherited pain, for we would know that our life's rhythm beats from Her great heart, torn with the agony of love and birth. And we would feel that death meant reunion with Her, a passing back into Her substance, blood of Her blood again, peace of Her peace!" It seems that it is not so much God that is rejected here as man's conventional notion of God. One is reminded in this connection of what Gabriel Marcel, the French philosopher, once said: "When we speak of God, it is not God of whom we speak." Regardless of how we judge the psychological plausibility of such speeches, they clearly represent one of O'Neill's many attempts to grapple with the problem of belief in a world from which God, as he saw it, had withdrawn.

Men In Nina's Life: By the time the curtain falls on Act Two, the audience has been introduced to all the men in Nina Leeds' life, with one important exception, the son who is not yet born and who will appear in the later acts of the play. These men, who enable Nina at different times in her life to fulfill a number of needs and to play a wide range of feminine roles are, just to summarize:

Gordon - potential lover and husband; both roles thwarted by death.

Professor Leeds - father; taken by death.

Marsden - father substitute; a role created by death of real father.

Evans - husband to be.

Darrell - like Trofimov in Chekhov's *The Cherry Orchard*, he fancies himself "about love." As a scientist, he strives for clinical detachment, yet we get some hints that he is drawn to Nina. As she informs Charles, "But once he kissed me - in a moment of carnal weakness!" He is Nina's lover-to-be.

Nina lacks only one other man-woman relationship, that of mother to son, a void which will be filled in the later stages of the play's action.

STRUGGLE AGAINST DEATH: A HOPE DASHED

Act Three, with its change of milieu, seems, at least at the start, to carry forward the possibilities for hope suggested at the end of Act Two. One can infer that the new setting, the Evans farm in upstate New York, as contrasted with the death-infected study of Professor Leeds, is the playwright's symbolic hint that Nina has begun her struggle to escape the emotional morass which up till now has threatened to engulf her life. She is now married to the healthy, robust, uncomplicated Sam Evans, the man who was raised on a farm. The note of hope seems further strengthened when we discover that Nina is expecting a child. The general elation created by the playwright in the beginning of the act is, however, quickly destroyed when Sam's mother tells Nina that the Evans family is infected with hereditary insanity. We are left with a feeling of hopelessness as the act ends with Nina agreeing to an abortion as she and Sam's mother fall weeping into each other's arms.

BRIEF CHARACTER ANALYSIS

1. Nina, when we first encounter her in Act Three, has undergone, some profound changes since last we saw her. She is physically fuller and healthier looking; she radiates an inner calm. The reason for these changes in her person, we discover, is that she is expecting a child, a fact which seems to hold the promise of happiness for her for the first time in her life. Bearing Sam's child will even help her, she feels, to come to love her husband. By the time the curtain falls on Act Three, however, Nina's hopes have been dashed, her brief moment of happiness has been obliterated by the revelation of hereditary insanity in the Evans family. She moves in this act from the heights of joy to the depths of despair.

2. Marsden suspects Nina's pregnancy. He is still strongly attracted to her, still neurotically fearful of the sexual facts of life.

3. Sam Evans is buoyantly optimistic about his business future, even though at the moment he is barely on the bottom rung of the ladder. Unaware of Nina's pregnancy, he is looking forward hopefully to their having a child. Like the other characters in this act, Sam in his dialogue and soliloquies helps to focus our attention upon the central issue of this act: Nina's pregnancy and her fateful, desperate decision to abort the fetus in order to break the cycle of insanity in the Evans line.

4. Mrs. Evans, who appears only in this act, is the Cassandra, the messenger of doom. It is she who reveals the dark secret hidden in the family's past. Herself a victim of the Evans curse, she is a tired old woman whose only aim in

life is to prevent Sam from being unhappy. With single-minded tenacity she persuades Nina not to give birth to the child she is carrying. She also suggests to Nina the possibility of her bearing a child by another man and passing it off as Sam's. This seed planted by Mrs. Evans is to bear fruit in the ensuing acts of the play.

Comment

Modern Equivalent Of Fate: It has been remarked that science, with its discovery of the influence of heredity and environment upon human behavior, has provided a modern counterpart of Fate, of what the Greeks called moira. The behaviorist social sciences, such as psychology, have done much through their deterministic emphases to strengthen the assumption that man's freedom is diminished by forces outside of himself over which he has no control. For the modern writer of tragedy who sees man's freedom threatened and perhaps even destroyed, the dignity, the meaning, the beauty, of human existence is to be achieved only in the struggle against an oppressive psychic and social environment, against what many feel to be a hostile, absurd universe. It is the way in which man faces his destiny that imparts meaning to life. In the words of Albert Camus, "Man is born to be defeated, but not to be destroyed."

Nina As Tragic Heroine: It is within some such perspective as this that we might examine the tragic condition to which Nina Leeds seems doomed. The victim of cruel tricks of fate, driven by psychic anxieties and feelings of guilt, she is certainly more sinned against than sinning. The disclosure in Act Three that she bears within her womb a child genetically destined for insanity crushes her, drives her into the depths of despair, but it does not destroy her. She has the quality of what Eugene O'Neill once called, in another context, "hopeless hope." She decides to fight back, according to her lights and within the severely limited area of freedom still available to her. It is this refusal to surrender passively to a hostile destiny which gives stature and dignity to Nina Leeds. In rejecting the peaceful oblivion of surrender, in continuing to clutter things up with that dirty thing called hope, to paraphrase Anouilh's heroine Antigone, Nina becomes something more than the pathetic subject of a clinical case study, as many people have been inclined to see her.

Sentimental Melodrama? Some will question whether O'Neill has actually succeeded in infusing his heroine with this kind of tragic, heroic dignity. It must be admitted that the playwright has in this act come perilously close to the bathos and sentimentality of melodrama. The ingredients of Act Three are the stuff of soap opera, and a good deal depends upon the taste, discipline, and control of the director and his actors if *Strange Interlude* is to avoid wallowing in sensationalism and gratuitous emotional titillation. It is possible, however, through disciplined artistry and underplaying, to raise the action to a higher plane of meaning. The curtain scene, for example, can be played "with all stops out," squeezing every last drop of emotional mileage from the suffering; The actresses must, however, reject this temptation. They must endeavor, through controlled playing, to lift the scene to the level of power and dignity that one finds, for instance, in the powerful final curtain of Chekhov's *Three Sisters*, which finds the three women locked in each other's arms, silently weeping. If Act Three does in fact have this potentiality for theatrical power when played correctly - and I believe it does - then O'Neill cannot be charged with having written a piece of sentimental melodrama. The dramatist is, after all, entitled to expect that his work will receive the most respectful artistic attention from all connected with the production.

Ghosts Of The Past: There is something Ibsenesque about Act Three, with its emphasis upon the ghosts of the past returning to haunt the present. The echoes of Ibsen's *Ghosts* are strong throughout this act, and not simply because of the hereditary insanity which looms so large in both plays. The memories of the great Norwegian's play are present in such a passage as the following description of the Evans house in Nina's letter to Darrell: "I feel it has lost its soul and grown resigned to doing without it. It isn't haunted by anything at all - and ghosts of some sort are the only normal life a house has - like our minds, you know."

It should be observed, finally, that Act Three offers a new variation on what might be regarded as the play's central **theme**, which can be stated in a number of ways: birth versus death, parents versus children, fertility versus sterility, the struggle against what Nina calls in Act Two "our trifling misery of death-born-of birth."

THE SELECTION OF A MATE

The clean, well-lighted tomb which we encountered as the setting for the first two acts becomes once again the mise en scene for Act Four - but with a significant difference. Instead of the strict order of the late Professor Leeds' study, we now find a disarray in the midst of which an unkempt Sam Evans sits trying futilely to write advertising copy. The contrast is dramatically sharp. Once again the playwright seems concerned to underline, through the visual impact of his set, the meaning of the play's action. The physical untidiness of the once sacrosanct library suggests the emotional and spiritual untidiness of Nina's life: her husband is failing at his work; she has had an abortion (unknown to Sam, who knew neither about her pregnancy nor the hereditary insanity in his family); and she and Sam are sexually estranged. She stays with Sam, one feels, only out of a sense of obligation - a legacy she has inherited from a severe New England upbringing, a contact with her late fiancé's "code of honor," and Mrs. Evans' lecture to her in the preceding act on the subject of Nina's obligation to her husband.

However, the audience, along with Nina, is provided with a new sense of quickening hope - as well as with the probability of new conflicts and problems - by the arrival of the attractive, virile young doctor, Ned Darrell. The playwright, we discover upon reflection, has skillfully planted the seed of our sense of expectation earlier in the play. Darrell has already struck us - if only unconsciously - as a strong, authoritative figure. His reemergence in the action at this point provides a dramatically strong contrast to the weak, ineffectual Sam Evans. Our sense of expectation is further strengthened when we add to these facts our remembrance of some advice Sam's mother had given Nina in the preceding act. The advice was that Nina should conceive a child by another man, unknown to Sam, and pass it off as Sam's as a way of making him happy and of possibly averting the insanity which hangs over his head. It becomes clear fairly quickly that Nina has decided upon Dr. Darrell as the man who will father her child. Darrell, mesmerized by Nina's magnetism, succumbs, and, under the guise of conducting a scientific experiment, he sobbingly agrees to Nina's plan as the curtain falls.

BRIEF CHARACTER ANALYSIS

1. Sam is working, ironically, in Professor Leeds' old study, futilely and desperately trying to write advertising copy. He is harassed and haunted by fears of failure. Nina's

strangeness, her illness, her distance from him, have added to his anxieties.

2. Nina's soliloquy reveals her contempt for Sam's weaknesses and failures. It is a contempt softened somewhat by pity but not by love. Distraught and bitter over the abortion, which Sam knows nothing about, she is obviously psychologically ripe for the strong, virile Doctor Darrell, whom she persuades in this act to become the father of her child.

3. Darrell's cool mastery and authoritative control meet their match and receive a check in the person of Nina, who skillfully uses all of her womanly powers to subdue the man she has singled out to father her child. Her motives are sexual need, the drive of her powerful maternal instinct, and her wish to make Sam happy by presenting him with a child which he will innocently accept as his own.

4. Marsden's role in this act is minimal. He comments wryly on Sam's contamination of Professor Leeds' study, and he also aids in the exposition by his intuitive awareness that Nina has had an abortion. His unnatural attachment to his mother and his refusal to accept reality are further underlined for us as we observe his panic at Darrell's suggestion that his ailing mother should receive medical attention.

Comment

Just as he has been doing in the preceding acts, O'Neill once again carefully prepares the entrance of a major character in the act, in this case Ned Darrell. Through the skillful juxtaposition of the attractive young doctor with the weak, unsuccessful Evans and the prim writer who is still tied to his mother, the playwright makes the audience quickly and dramatically aware of Darrell's strength and virility. Doctor Darrell is clearly a strong candidate for the role of the "healthy male" theoretically discussed in the preceding act as the potential father of Nina's child. He is a successful scientist (a prestige-laden profession in our culture); he is confidently in control of virtually every situation in which he finds himself. He is intellectually dominating and coolly self-assertive, almost to the point of arrogance. As it turns out, however, he is no match for Nina Leeds, who becomes in this act O'Neill's dark counterpart of Shaw's single-minded heroine Ann Whitfield, the embodiment of "the life force" in the play *Man and Superman*.

Darrell And Nina: It is clear from the moment they confront one another that Ned and Nina, who have not met since her marriage, are still strongly attracted to each other. Darrell's sexual magnetism cannot be concealed behind the protective facade of cool, clinical detachment he has constructed around his emotional life. Nina, who has become vibrantly alive upon seeing her old friend once again, tells him early in their conversation, "You're the taking kind for whom opportunities are made!" Although the statement is directed at Ned's success in his profession, the words obviously operate, whether consciously or not, on another level and constitute an indirect offering of herself to him. Both characters in different ways attempt to conceal, from themselves and from each other, that they are powerfully drawn to each other, although as the scene progresses Nina is less and less concerned to hide her true intentions. It becomes clear too that Nina's pursuit of Darrell is at least as much the result of her instinctive maternal need for a child as of her sexual need for an attractive male.

The Fiction Of Scientific Detachment: The entire seduction scene, if it may be called that, is conducted as a pathetically transparent **parody** of a doctor-patient relationship. Nina calls him "Doctor" throughout the scene, until the very end when, speaking of herself and of him in the third person, she says, "Ned always attracted her." Darrell's inner thoughts, revealed in the asides, disclose the turbulent state of his emotions, a turbulence which he attempts to bury beneath the cool professionalism of his external manner. It is the contrast between the spoken dialogue and his "unspoken" inner thoughts that provides the dramatic counterpoint of the scene. Under Nina's relentless pursuit Darrell's scientific urbanity inevitably shatters, although right down to the end he keeps up the by now feeble pretense of clinical detachment. It has been clear throughout, however, that he has all along been more than a willing candidate for the role of Nina's mate. His fictional pose fools no one, least of all himself.

LOVE-HATE-POWER

Once again the discerning spectator (or reader) will respond to the muted symbolism of the mise en scene of Act Five: the setting is a house near the sea, the eternal symbol of birth and life, and the time is April, that time of year when the earth is reborn. It is a most appropriate context in which to situate the play's heroine, now a pregnant Nina, carrying Ned Darrell's child in her womb. Sam, even shabbier than he was in the preceding act, is not only unaware that he has been cuckolded by Darrell - he doesn't even know that his wife is pregnant. One has the sense, as one observes this tragically entangled web of human relationships, that human love is indeed a complex emotion. Nina's whole life - her drives, her needs, her failures - can be viewed as the pitiful attempt to come to terms with her inadequate sense of love. For her, to love is to control, to manipulate, to possess. Charles Marsden, who hovers morosely over the play's entire action, is afraid of love, is both attracted and repelled by Nina, is contemptuous of her husband, and is openly hostile to Darrell, whom he intuitively knows to be Nina's lover. Darrell, in turn, who tries to play the role of the detached scientist, is fearful of any human involvement, and alternately loves and hates the woman who has paralyzed his will.

Act Five is a series of explorations of these shifting, complicated relationships, culminating in Darrell's informing Sam of Nina's pregnancy (without, of course, revealing the real facts about the parentage). Sam is overjoyed, ironically, at the news that he is about to become a father. Nina, however, is crushed, since she had planned to tell Sam the truth and then run off with her lover. Darrell, for his part, flees to Europe, where, he hopes that a life of dissipation will drown his memories and his love of Nina. One is overcome, as the act ends, by a sense of hopelessness concerning Nina's ability to achieve happiness herself or to bring it to others.

BRIEF CHARACTER ANALYSIS

1. Evans is shabby and even more despondent than in the preceding act, for he is now jobless. Ned Darrell, feeling remorse as well as pity for this weak man whom he has cuckolded, offers to help Sam in finding a job. Evans is clearly at the nadir of his existence and even thinks vaguely about suicide.

2. Nina is radiantly happy since she is once again expecting a child, this time Darrell's. She is unable to conceal her contempt for her ineffectual husband. She is still

attempting to coerce Darrell to do her bidding - to take her away from Sam and marry her. Her hold over him, however, is almost exclusively physical, and she is unable to control him once he is out of her presence.

3. Darrell, who since the end of Act Four has become Nina's lover, has mixed feelings toward her. He is still powerfully attracted to her, but there is a part of him which hates her. He is, furthermore, torn by feelings of guilt at having deceived his old friend Sam Evans.

Comment

Offstage Events: It is interesting to observe how much of the action in this play occurs offstage between the acts. The dramatist, who like any artist must select those details he wishes to weave into a meaningful whole, must also, by the same token, exclude certain items. This need for economy of selection forces the writer to report rather than present certain events and actions directly on the stage. In this play the primary focus of O'Neill's attention is the conflict arising out of the psychological states of his characters, and he is, consequently, less interested in the events themselves than in the characters' preparations for and responses to the pressures of those events. A brief list of some of the key actions which take place either in the pre-curtain life of the play or between the acts would include: Gordon's death, Professor Leeds' death, Nina's sexual promiscuity at the hospital, her marriage to Sam, her abortion, the physical consummation of her love affair with Darrell, the death of Marsden's mother. Reported offstage action is, it will be recalled, a dramatic **convention** as old as Greek tragedy.

Nina's Attempts To Control Darrell: The dramatic center of this act is the struggle between Nina and Darrell. Nina, whose woman role is now that of desirable mistress, is shortly to enter into a new phase of her womanliness. She is about to become the woman-as-mother, and she is using every seductive weapon in her power to tie firmly to her the man who has fathered her unborn child. The original intention (half real, half pretext) of entering into the liaison with Darrell only to make Sam happy has now been shelved. She announces to Darrell, "I'm going to be happy! I've lost everything in life so far because I didn't have the courage to take it - and I've hurt everyone around me. There's no use trying to think of others. One human being can't think of another. It's impossible. But this time I'm going to think of my own happiness - and that means you - and our child!" Darrell, momentarily blinded by his passionate desire for Nina, thinks of "the touch of her soft skin...those afternoons! ...God, I was happy." A moment later he feebly surrenders with the words, "Yes, Nina." The moment he is removed from Nina's dominating physical presence, however, he regains his will: motivated by his own selfish careerism, his fears of permanent entanglement with Nina, and his guilt over betraying his friend Sam, he rushes off to Europe, to plunge once again into the antiseptic world of scientific research, a world that remains untouched and uncomplicated by the demands of people.

NINA AND HER MEN: LOVE AS DOMINATION

As the curtain rises for the beginning of Act Six, we find ourselves looking in on what appears to be a scene of domestic, middle-class bliss. Nina is now a mother; Sam, motivated by a son he mistakenly takes to be his own, has become a complacently confident, successful businessman; Marsden, the eternal friend of the family and dabbler in literature, still patiently worships Nina from the sidelines; Ned Darrell, the absent lover in this ménage a quatre, has been living in Europe, but returns during this act, drawn irresistibly by the magnetic Nina. But before he returns, Marsden jealously lashes out at Nina, still trying to fathom the truth of what he has guessed - Nina's and Darrell's extra-marital love affair. Marsden, it should be recalled, has been mourning the death of his mother, the figure in his life from whom he had never been able to free himself. The sense of calm pervading the household is, in short, more apparent than real. The return of Ned Darrell - pale, thin, weakened by dissipation and despair - signals the renewal and further development of the complex personal relationships and conflicts which form the dramatic core of the play.

Standing at the center of the labyrinth of human relationships is, of course, Nina, the tormented figure who strives to become the quintessential woman. It is fairly obvious that the tormented need to become all things to all men stems from those psychic scars which have radically marred her ability to love. Her need for love has been twisted into a self-destructive drive to dominate totally all of the men in her life. For one moment, however, at the end of this act, she seems to have achieved the precarious and psychologically impossible position of holding all the men in her life in a delicate, transfixed state of equilibrium and submission: Sam, the worshipping husband; Charles Marsden, the ambivalent father figure who adores her quietly and patiently, waiting for her ultimately to turn to him; Ned Darrell, the dispirited lover, who is drawn to Nina in spite of himself; and, finally, the newcomer on the scene, Nina's year old son, asleep upstairs, the child who is the product of Nina's illicit love affair with her lover-healer, Darrell. The act ends in the kind of silent, tableau-like action which the Elizabethans called a dumb show. Each of the characters speaks a soliloquy, and the action concludes with Nina going to each of the seated men in turn and kissing them: Sam as she might affectionately kiss a big brother, Charles as she might dutifully kiss her father, and Darrell lovingly on the lips as she would kiss her lover.

BRIEF CHARACTER ANALYSIS

1. Sam Evans has undergone a radical transformation since we last saw him. Nina has borne a son whom he mistakenly takes to be his own. This has given him the self-confidence he so badly lacked and facilitated his entering upon the path of worldly, financial success. His newly found confidence has won him the respect of his wife, and he now oozes the contentment of the happy husband, the proud father, and the successful businessman.

2. Nina has aged. She is calm, contented in her motherhood, but not really happy. Darrell's return in this act from his self-imposed exile in Europe brings back a spark of vitality into her life. We see her at the end of the act supremely but ephemerally triumphant, surrounded by all of her men. She has become the All-Woman - if only for a moment.

3. Darrell is at the low point of his life. His attempts to drown his love for Nina in a sea of dissipation have merely aged and embittered him. His career virtually destroyed, his life a meaningless void, he returns, a pathetic figure, to kneel suppliantly at Nina's feet.

4. Charles Marsden, who seems always to be present, bitterly resents Nina's past entanglement with Darrell, an entanglement which the novelist had guessed. Darrell's sudden, unexpected return in this act unleashes in Marsden a flood of bitterness directed at the hapless doctor. Still patiently in love with Nina, Marsden feels that he alone can care for and protect her.

Comment

Strong Curtains: All of the curtain scenes in *Strange Interlude* are dramatically strong, some more so than others. It will be recalled that the first five acts end, respectively, on the following climactic notes: Act One with the Professor movingly looking ahead to his impending death; Act Two with Marsden carrying the sleeping Nina offstage and laughing bitterly to the contrapuntal accompaniment of Sam's bland comments; Act Three ends with Nina and her mother-in-law weeping in each other's arms; Act Four with Darrell's passionate acceptance of Nina's invitation to father her child; Act Five ends with Nina, pregnant and deserted by her lover, bleakly holding her husband's head to her breast and looking forward to a joyless, loveless future. These are strong scenes, representing high points of emotional intensity that have been carefully built up by the dramatist. The curtain scene in Act Six is, however, probably the most theatrically effective thus far in the play, and rightly so, since this represents the pinnacle, the **climax** of the play's action. There is an almost tableau-like quality about the scene, a quality that one can visualize being powerfully heightened by effective staging and lighting. The surface quality of the action is static as each of the four characters in turn soliloquizes in aria-like fashion. The scene is visually as well as verbally a theatrical

metaphor for the quiet plateau of feminine fulfillment which Nina has attained.

Nina As Outsized Heroine: O'Neill's heroine, by the end of Act Six, has achieved a larger-than-life status; she has taken on qualities that are almost mythical in dimension and scope. She has fulfilled virtually all the roles and functions available to a woman, and as she stands surrounded by the men in her life, she has become a modern Everywoman. Her inner musings reveal her, for the moment at least, more as the embodiment of womanliness than as this particular woman, Nina Leeds Evans: "My three men! ...I feel their desires converge in me!... to form one complete beautiful male desire which I absorb... and am whole...they dissolve in me, their life is my life...I am pregnant with the three! ...husband! ...lover! ...father! ...little Gordon! ...he is mine too!...that makes it perfect!" One might see here a fulfillment of the role she had vaguely but prophetically envisioned for herself in Act One, when she declared, "I've been becoming myself. And I must finish!" She has not, however, completely transcended the particularity of her flesh-and-blood existence as Nina Leeds Evans. She has not, in short, become an abstraction, a feminine principle and nothing more, as some of O'Neill's critics have charged. The starkly simple, quietly moving ritual of the three kisses which ends the act reminds the audience that this woman before our eyes is indeed simultaneously Sam's husband, Darrell's lover, Marsden's daughter/mother substitute, and young Gordon's mother. Nina, it might be said, is a lot of woman.

Indictment Of Society's Values: Act Six, as it moves along to the climactic moment discussed above, manages to include O'Neill's strong indictment of certain values on which American society is based. He achieves this primarily through Marsden's scathing reflections on Sam Evans as symbol of American success. He comments, for example, "His is an adolescent mind...he'll never grow up...well, in this adolescent country, what greater blessing could he wish for?" And a moment or two later he adds, thinking to himself, "What a fount of meaningless energy he's tapped! ...always on the go...typical terrible child of the age...universal slogan, keep moving...moving where? ...never mind that...don't think of ends...the means are the end...keep moving! ...It's in every headline of this daily newer testament...going...going... never mind the gone...we won't live to see it...and we'll be so rich, we can buy off the deluge anyway! ...even our new God has His price! ...must have! ...aren't we made in His image? ...or vice versa?" Marsden himself, although he serves here as the vehicle through which the playwright articulates his value judgments, is also attacked at other points in the action as the shallow, withdrawn artist who has substituted word lies for life. It might be remembered too that Darrell, as the symbolic embodiment of the scientific world view or, more accurately of scientism, is also condemned as one whose values are sterile and inadequate. It is clear that although O'Neill had, prior to his writing *Strange Interlude*, announced his withdrawal from social and political concerns, he was nevertheless still interested, perhaps in a profounder way than before, in his world and its behavior. He was, in a very real sense, the playwright as moralist, a role which no literary artist can really avoid playing.

WOMAN AS MOTHER

O'Neill, in his relentlessly probing, yet sympathetic study of a neurotic modern woman, seems intent upon laying bare those wellsprings of emotional Angst and inadequacy which drive Nina Leeds from man to man, from role to role, in her quest for womanly fulfillment. Our discovery of Nina's inner being is a gradual one. We participate in this discovery along with her creator as we follow her on her tormented journey through life. O'Neill's method of revelation is not the clinical one of the psychologist; it is the artistic method of the dramatist who creates and reveals his character through action-which is, after all, a definition of drama as ancient as Aristotle's *Poetics*. In Act Seven, for example, we see Nina presiding over the celebration of her son's eleventh birthday in their plush Park Avenue apartment. She is now totally and exclusively woman-as-mother. Ned, her former lover, is a bitter, disillusioned hanger-on who sporadically returns to her from a biology research station in the West Indies. Ned and Nina quarrel briefly, kiss and make up, but as they embrace, Nina's son Gordon sees them and is shocked. Gordon instinctively hates this man, but he loves the eternally present Charles Marsden and, of course, Sam, who he mistakenly regards as his true father. Nina, for her part, has contempt for all three men, centering all of her possessive love on the son who is, we infer, the reincarnation of Nina's dead lover-hero, Gordon Shaw.

BRIEF CHARACTER ANALYSIS

1. This time it is Ned Darrell who has bounced back dramatically from the lower depths. His recovery, however, is only partial, since he bears about him the bitter emotional wounds and scars of his affair with Nina. He has patched up his broken life and career to some extent: he is financially successful, he has taken up a new scientific career, but he has not been able to shake the hold which Nina still retains over his emotional life. He periodically returns to the woman who has been at once the source of his happiness and his misery. He is on the whole, however, a bitter, disillusioned man.

2. Nina has become the mother, totally and exclusively so. At this stage in her life she has no need for the three men in her life: Evans, Darrell, Marsden. Her entire existence is centered about her eleven-year-old son, whom she has named after the dead hero, Gordon Shaw.

3. Marsden is openly quite hostile toward Darrell, since Marsden's unflagging love for Nina has produced strong feelings of jealousy toward the man who was once her lover.

4. Sam Evans is the embodiment of self-satisfaction, a congenial bon vivant who delights in the simple adoration of "his" son Gordon. Evans continues to hero-worship Nina's dead fiancé, and he tells the young boy stories about the dead Gordon's legendary athletic exploits. It is clear that his influence over the boy is destined to mold a second Gordon Shaw, who will be successful like Sam and heroic like the dead flier.

Comment

Haunted By The Past: The eleven-year interlude between the end of Act Six and the opening of Act Seven has wrought many changes in the lives of this strangely interlocked group of characters. It might be more accurate to describe the new situation as not so much the product of change, but as the culmination of certain lines of development irrevocably set in motion by earlier events. Each character, taken alone and also in relationship to the others, is clearly the product of their collective past. Most of them are haunted by the ghosts of that past. Darrell is embittered at having lost his son to Evans and also at his twilight existence as far as Nina is concerned. He has neither completely won nor completely lost this woman he continues to love. Nina sees this too, thinking to herself that he has "never had the courage to insist on all or nothing." Darrell does not even have the solace of his work to console him, for he is now little more than a dabbler in science, "a scientific dilettante," as Marsden puts it. The great "scientific experiment" (of making Sam happy by presenting him with a healthy child) has not been carried out with the necessary cold-blooded objectivity. Human feelings have intervened to clutter up the experimental laboratory. Darrell, unable to live happily with or without Nina as things stand, has been emotionally destroyed, envying Evans his fatuous success, scorning Marsden as a prissy, womanish writer of genteel novels. His unacknowledged son's closeness to both Evans and Marsden is an impossibly bitter pill to swallow, and he retreats abjectly to a life of science which no longer holds any meaning for him.

Marsden's Love For Nina: Marsden, still afraid of life, manages to avoid most of it by hiding behind the artificial, passionless world of his novels. Living now with his sister, he still yearns for Nina, trying to convince himself that his love for her includes nothing of desire. Nina thinks of him, portentously, as her "dear old Charlie," and of "what a perfect lover he would make for one's old age...a perfect lover when one was past passion." A second later, however, Nina reflects to herself, "These men make me sick! ... I hate all three of them! ... They disgust me!...the wife and mistress in me has been killed by them!" Her feelings are softened by remorse, since, as she muses at another time, "I have wounded everyone."

The Successful Evans: Sam Evans alone seems to have thrived in this tangled web of destructive relationships. He is happy-or at least content-in his health, prosperity, and family. Ironically, the potentially sick, beaten, weak Sam Evans of the earlier acts has become the swaggeringly successful man of Act Seven. As Darrell cynically puts it, "The huge joke has dawned on me! ...Sam is the only normal one!...we lunatics! ...Nina and I!" Even here, however, we are never allowed to forget that the surface success is built upon a foundation of lies, and that Sam Evans is, in reality, another hollow man. The tableau-like pageant which ended the preceding act has, predictably, been shattered. Human lives and emotions do not, after all, stand still, the way they do in a tableau. Nina's selfish, one might even say ruthless, attempt to possess and control the three men in her life contained a built-in guarantee of destruction.

Nina And The Future: Nina's past has mangled and scarred her, her present life is marred by the memories, guilt, and human relics of that past, and she has only the future to live and hope for. Her son Gordon is that future, but already we notice the presentiments, the danger signs of trouble to come. The trouble is undoubtedly inherent in the very nature of Nina's love. It is a love which, in its possessiveness, in its need to control, denies freedom to the other, and finally must suffocate both herself and the object of her love. She has moved, in Act Seven, into yet another phase of her womanhood, sloughing off the other, earlier phases as a snake would its old skin. She is now the Mother, and her whole life is centered about her son. The development and completion of this final man-woman role in her life will take up the concluding two acts of the play.

COUNTERPOINT: A VICTORY AND A FINAL DEFEAT

Time moves relentlessly on. One generation gives way to another, retreating sadly, emptily to life's sidelines, making room for offspring it neither understands nor possesses. For Nina not to possess is the kind of lethal blow she cannot survive.

Her son, now twenty-one, no longer needs her, and, finishing his career in a blaze of athletic glory, is about to embark on a new life with his fiancée, Madeline Arnold. Nina, inevitably, looks upon this young girl as an intrusive rival for Gordon's love. Act Eight, which takes place on the afterdeck of a launch from which the characters view Gordon's last varsity crew race, witnesses Nina's final struggle for power. Her husband-stout, prosperous, adolescently eager and opinionated-no longer seems infatuated by the woman he married. Ned too seems to have extricated himself from her tentacles, and he successfully resists Nina's efforts to entangle him once more. She is resolved somehow to enlist Darrell's aid in winning Gordon away from Sam and, more importantly, from her love rival, Madeline.

Her objective throughout this act, consequently, is to stir up whatever embers of Darrell's old love for her may still be smoldering. Since his objective is to retain his new-found freedom by avoiding the magnetic power of Nina's powerful will, the dramatic struggle between these two is very intense and dominates this act. Darrell proclaims his intention of never again meddling with any life possessing more than a single cell. He is able to look calmly into Nina's eyes without feeling desire, jealousy, or bitterness. His resistance begins to waver, however, as Nina begins to cast her old, hypnotic spell of the flesh over him, stirring old memories of desire and love. Nina wants her old lover to support her in telling Sam the truth about Gordon's parentage in a last, desperate effort to win back her son. Darrell is tempted, and weakens momentarily under her power, but the sudden, brief appearance of an intoxicated Marsden breaks the spell and releases Darrell from Nina's clutching tentacles. There seems to be no one left now for Nina but the patient cipher, Charles Marsden. She does in fact turn to him, revealing the whole truth about her son's true father and asking Marsden's forgiveness. This man, the audience sees as Act Eight ends, is

Nina's final haven, especially since the act concludes with Sam lying prostrate on the deck, felled by an apparently fatal stroke brought on by the excitement of his son's victory.

BRIEF CHARACTER ANALYSIS

1. Sam Evans, still jovial and simple, has grown independent of his wife, whose moodiness he finds destructive of that atmosphere of conviviality which he wishes at all times to surround him. His life, now that he has achieved financial success, seems to consist totally in the vicarious enjoyment he derives from young Gordon's athletic prowess and the prospects of the young man's happy marriage to Madeline Arnold, a pretty young girl who resembles Nina when she was that age.

2. Darrell, still filled with bitterness and leading a life of disappointed loneliness, has regained some of his old self-mastery. His detachment now bears traces of the cynicism which his unhappy life has bred in him. He has finally broken the spell which Nina had cast over him.

3. Nina seems to be devoid of feeling, very much as we found her in act two, with one crucial exception. She is driven now solely and destructively by a need to possess and control the one remaining love object in her life. This neurotic need to possess, this inability to share her son's love, compels her to attempt to drive a wedge between the twenty-one-year-old Gordon and the girl he is soon to marry. She is a bitter, lonely, aging woman, desperately grasping at what she considers to be her last opportunity for any kind of human love.

4. Charles Marsden, who has aged greatly, is still waiting patiently for Nina. He is in perpetual mourning for his deceased mother and for his sister, who has recently died.

Comment

Nina's Final Struggle: In Act Eight we witness Nina's last struggle for power and her final defeat. Driven by a compulsive need to possess and control her love objects, she has never been able, since the traumatic shock of Gordon Shaw's death, to experience the love which leads to freedom and growth. The sole male object left in her life is her son, and the prospect of losing him to Madeline Arnold drives her to a desperate but futile attempt to retain him in her possession. Her desire to control and manipulate is, in some way, associated with a maternal, creative urge which has taken a strange theological twist. For her, womanliness, motherhood, imply and demand a rejection of God the Father and an attempt to raise herself as a rival Mother God in a struggle for power. The creative act of motherhood has in this play taken on the dimensions of a titanic, Manichean struggle between two contending forces for control of the universe. (At least one critic has seen significance in the fact that the heroine's name, Nina, and the number of acts in the play, nine, happen to coincide with the gestation period before the birth of a child.) The psychological roots of Nina's rejection of the father as an authority figure are clearly established in the play and have already been touched upon. Darrell, once again to some extent the detached observer, cautions Nina in this act, "You've got to give up owning people, meddling in their lives as if you were God and had created them!" Nina, who throughout the play has never really been able to face the reality of the present, still lives haunted by the memory of the past and pathetically driven by a desperate hope that the future will bring happiness and peace. The play's entire action can, in a sense, be viewed as the psychic grinding of Nina between the twin stones of memory and hope. She herself reflects, in a passage which gives the play its title, "The only living life is in the past and future... the present is an interlude...strange interlude in which we call on past and future to bear witness we are living!"

Strange Interlude: To put the matter slightly differently, between the two poles which mark off the action of this play- between Nina's rejection of her father in Act One and her return to the father, Marsden, in the last act-we have the span of time which sees the ascent, the brief, hollow triumph, and the defeat of Nina. This stretch of time is the strange interlude of struggle between those resting points of peace, oblivion, death.

Cyclic Return: It is this cyclic return to the past, this ritual of psychic repetition and regression, which to a large extent gives the play its shape and design, as well as its fatalistic sense of tragedy. The motif of cyclic repetition is especially strong in this act. For one thing, Gordon, whose ghost has dominated and guided so much of the play's actions, has come back to life in his namesake, the athlete-hero Gordon Evans. Nina we find once again trying to possess a Gordon, and once again she finds her efforts doomed to failure, just as similar efforts had failed her in the past. Darrell is, as we have seen, once more the detached scientific observer whom we encountered earlier in the play. The major difference is, ironically, his refusal now to "meddle," a refusal based on a wisdom he has gained through bitter experience. His previous attempts to interfere with and to guide the lives of others (arranging Nina's marriage to Sam and later fathering Nina's child) have produced only bitterness and destruction. Sam Evans, by the end of this act, has been literally brought low, has been reduced to the emotionally neutral cipher he was when we first met him. Marsden once again emerges in this act as Nina's father figure, and in a confessional scene strongly and deliberately reminiscent of its counterpart in Act Two, Nina regresses to a dependent childlike state, confesses her sins and asks for forgiveness. She has never faced the present; the future no longer holds any hope for her; there remains to her only the past, into which she now crawls for comfort and security.

Cyclic Return As Form: The cyclic quality of much of Act Eight gives *Strange Interlude* a symmetry of structure, an architectonic form which buttresses or in a real sense is the play's central meaning. Whatever else may be said - and much can be - about the play's inflated rhetoric, its heavy Freudian apparatus, its ponderous attempts to achieve the status of myth in modern dress, it must be conceded that *Strange Interlude* is marked by that one trait without which a work of art ceases to be art: shape, pattern, design, form.

TWILIGHT OF THE GODDESS

A calm seems to have descended, but it is the stillness of the tomb. Sam Evans' funeral has just taken place, Gordon is about to leave with Madeline, and Ned Darrell will shortly take his leave to return to his scientific work, never to return. Marsden, Nina's father substitute and the death figure of the play, alone remains. Everything, as far as Nina is concerned, reeks of death. Her acceptance of Charles Marsden's proposal of marriage represents the inevitability and finality of a woman's accepting defeat, ceasing to struggle, and submitting resignedly to the peaceful oblivion of death. The cycle is now completed. Nina has struggled to achieve love, to find and fulfill herself, and has lost the battle of life. There remains nothing but the nirvana of a death-in-life existence with a man who is both an unsuccessful novelist, and more significantly, an unsuccessful human being.

BRIEF CHARACTER ANALYSIS

1. Nina in this act ceases to struggle. Her last battle for love has ended in defeat and she retires from the fray, exhausted, finding quiet and peace in the arms of Marsden, her second father. Her loss of her son Gordon to Madeline marks the final phase of the strange interlude which has been her life. There is nothing left for her now but death, prefigured in her impending marriage to Marsden.

2. Marsden is quiet and serene in the triumphal achievement he had confidently waited for during so many years. The emotional calmness of his proposal to Nina has about it the stillness of death.

3. Darrell takes his final leave of Nina, never to see her again. The remainder of his life he will now devote totally to biological research, a field of investigation in which the only form of life one can meddle with is the single-celled variety.

Comment

Tying Up Loose ends: The concluding act is a brief one, its chief function being to tie up the remaining loose ends, in ways which were adequately forecast and prepared in the preceding act. O'Neill's performance of his final dramatist's task is not, however, carried out in a desultory, perfunctory fashion. Like any well-constructed dramatic scene, this final act has its own rhythm of conflict, building up to a peak of intensity and theatrical excitement, before leveling off and descending to the note of quiet restfulness on which the play ends. It represents, in its own way, the same kind of craftsman like symmetry and balance which characterizes the structure of the play as a whole. The play's action, if charted in linear fashion, would approximate a well constructed arch, resting on the two solid pillars of Acts One and Nine: the preparation for the struggle, or interlude, and the quiet aftermath of that struggle. Act Six (mathematical precision is not essential to the organic life of a work of art) is the keystone of the arch, for it is here, it will be recalled, that we find Nina at the zenith of her struggle with life and love, standing triumphantly surrounded by the men in her life. From that point on, Nina's fortunes descend, until at the play's end we find her symbolically embracing the oblivion of death in the person of the paternal death figure, Charles Marsden.

Act Nine, on a smaller scale, likewise rises to its **climax** and then falls off quietly. The dramatic high point is reached in the bitter outburst between Darrell and Gordon, the son he has never acknowledged as his own. The tension, which had quietly but steadily built up to this explosion, quickly dissolves, and in rapid succession Ned makes a final attempt to tell Gordon the truth, Nina prevents the disclosure, Gordon goes off to Madeline with his illusions about Evans and Nina intact, Darrell offers to marry Nina and is turned down, and Nina falls wearily into the arms of the patient, constant, ever-waiting Charles Marsden. O'Neill, with sure dramatic instincts, brings his action tidily and neatly to its conclusion in a remarkable display of theatrical economy and skill.

Son Versus Father: The simmering hostility between Gordon Evans and his real father, Ned Darrell, a hostility which erupts into physical violence in this last act, might be regarded as one more contribution to that great seminal archetype which has stood at the center of so much of primitive mythology, which has been the subject of so many great works of world literature (*Oedipus Rex*, *Hamlet*, *The Brothers Karamazov*, *Fathers and Sons*, *Vanity Fair*, *The Wild Duck*, Joyce's *Ulysses*, *All the King's Men*, to mention a few), and which has commanded the attention of many modern writers on psychoanalysis. The **theme** of the son rising up against the father is certainly not a new idea in the history of man nor in the literature he has produced. O'Neill, influenced by the intellectual climate that existed at the time he was writing *Strange Interlude*, has given a peculiarly, explicitly psychological twist to this pattern of conflict which, according to psychoanalytic theory, is profoundly rooted in both the racial and individual unconscious of man. The son is the father's rival for the mother's love, or as Nina expresses it in Act Nine, "Sons are always their fathers. They pass through the mother to become their father again."

Attempts At Poetry: Although, as we have seen, O'Neill's over-all craftsmanship in planning and building this final act was never surer, still there are weaknesses which cannot be ignored. The dramatist is striving in Act Nine to achieve a lyrical repose, a poetic calm. In seeking to verbalize the cathartic effects of the turbulent action of his play he attempts, here more than any place else in this work, to escape the flatness and banalities of realistic prose dialogue. The attempt is admirable, but O'Neill is straining after effects, he is trying too hard, and it shows. The result is "fine" writing, the hollow rhetoric of pseudo-poetry which many of O'Neill's critics have found offensive. Charles Marsden's opening soliloquy in this act provides a good example of O'Neill's frequent attempts to heighten language, attempts which too often merely inflate it: "My life is cool green shade wherein comes no scorching zenith sun of passion and possession to wither the heart with bitter poisons...my life gathers roses, coolly crimson, in sheltered gardens, on late afternoons in love with evening...roses heavy with after-blooming of the long day, desiring evening...my life is an evening... Nina is a rose, my rose, exhausted by the long, hot day, leaning wearily toward peace.... Nina and I have moved on to the moon." Literarily this passage just does not come off, and it is difficult to imagine it as anything but histrionically disastrous when delivered in the theater. Marsden's proposal to Nina is less pretentiously poetic, or perhaps it is merely briefer than the one just quoted: "We'll be married in the afternoon, decidedly. I've already picked out the church, Nina - a gray ivied chapel, full of restful shadow, symbolical of the peace we have found. The crimsons and purples in the windows will stain our faces with faded passion. It must be in the hour before sunset when the earth dreams in afterthoughts and mystic premonitions of life's beauty." The only possible excuse for such awkward, self-conscious attempts at prose-poetry is that Charles Marsden is a writer of bad novels and that he is probably talking, through most of Act Nine, like a character out of one of his own books.

End Of The Interlude: One of Marsden's speeches, like the others self-consciously studded with poetic **imagery**, does, despite its dramatic inappropriateness, suggest a perspective in which the entire play might be viewed, that is, as a series of purgative experiences by which the **protagonists** are cleansed by their sufferings: "There was something unreal," he advises Nina, "in all that has happened since you first met Gordon Shaw, something extravagant and fantastic, the sort of thing that isn't done, really, in our afternoons. So let's you and me forget the whole distressing **episode**, regard it as an interlude, of trial and preparation, say, in which our souls have been scraped clean of impure flesh and made worthy to bleach in peace." To which Nina replies, "Strange Interlude! Yes, our lives are merely strange dark interludes in the electrical display of God the Father!" The interlude, life, is over, bringing with it the restfulness of release, of death. As Nina reflects, in one of her soliloquies in this act, "I am sad but there's comfort in the thought that now I am free at last to rot away in peace." In returning to Marsden, she has come to terms with God the Father, but the note of apparent serenity and wistful surrender on which the play ends tells us that Nina, more than "half in love with easeful death," has finally given up the struggle which is life for the quiet stillness of the tomb.

STRANGE INTERLUDE

REVIEW OF CRITICISM

The first point to be made is that, on the question of O'Neill's achievement and final reputation, there is no consensus, nor is it likely that there ever will be. Rarely in the history of the drama have opinions been so widely and sharply divergent as in the case of Eugene O'Neill. Condemned as a well-intentioned yet clumsy writer with a penchant for experimenting but with nothing to say, and hailed as one of the theatrical giants of the century, this actor's son who wrote more than forty plays seems destined to remain a figure of permanent controversy. It is quite possible, of course, that when the dust of the present critical battle has settled and when a future generation of critics is able to avail itself of that comfortable, mystical condition known as "historical perspective," a true critical consensus may in fact arise. There are some signs, in fact, that the views of so balanced and influential a critic as John Gassner are already providing the basis for a more or less permanent evaluation of O'Neill's significance. Gassner, who is fully aware of the many obvious faults in O'Neill's work, is concerned to explore the roots of O'Neill's theatrical successes without soft-pedaling the failures. The playwright's output, as everyone concedes, was as uneven as it was prolific, and any sweeping judgment either in praise or in condemnation must be suspect by definition. The admitted unevenness of his work makes glib generalizations about that work impossible. Amidst the many shrill voices which have been raised for or against O'Neill's plays, John Gassner, who on the whole admires O'Neill and is inclined to see in him a measure of greatness, has been quietly attempting to assess and to demonstrate the sources of that greatness. Mr. Gassner is singled out here as a representative of the kind of balanced, nonpartisan critical judgment which seems likely to prevail when the strident voices have been stilled and when some sort of mixed consensus will have been reached.

International Discussion: In the meantime, the controversy over O'Neill's achievement rages on. The discussion has, for some years, been international in scope, an inevitable outcome of O'Neill's receiving the Nobel Prize as well as of the translation of many of his plays into many languages and their frequent production in foreign lands. (Three O'Neill plays actually had their world premieres outside the borders of America, in Stockholm, Sweden.) Books and articles on O'Neill have already been published in at least five languages. Most of O'Neill's negative critics, however, have been American. Europeans, on the whole (the British excepted), have tended to admire him.

The list of those who have written about Eugene O'Neill is impressive, in terms of both length and eminence. The list includes some or the finest critical and creative minds of this and the preceding generation. Despite the wide divergence of critical opinion concerning O'Neill's significance, one thing at any rate is clear. A writer who has evoked such widespread and high caliber responses cannot be ignored and undoubtedly will not be ignored by future generations. Eugene O'Neill's fame and permanence, it seems safe to say, seem secure, even though the precise nature and basis of that fame and permanence have still to be determined.

The Critical Lines: Before proceeding to a sampling of the critical responses to *Strange Interlude*, we might first attempt to suggest some of the lines which O'Neill criticism has tended to follow during the past thirty years or so. Obviously nothing even remotely approaching a full cross section of that criticism can be attempted within the limited space available here. What follows then can be nothing more than a hint, a skeletal outline of some of the major emphases and concerns which seem to have preoccupied those who have chosen to write about "America's major playwright." For purposes of convenience the critical opinions have been gathered under several headings: (1) O'Neill's over-all achievement and significance; (2) O'Neill as a craftsman of the theater; (3) the language of O'Neill's plays; (4) O'Neill's religious concerns as expressed in his plays; (5) O'Neill as a social critic; (6) O'Neill's interest in internal, psychological conflict. At the conclusion of this admittedly over-schematized survey of O'Neill criticism, a brief sampling of the critical commentary on *Strange Interlude* will be offered.

OVER-ALL ACHIEVEMENT

By the sheer force and weight of his impact on the American theater, Eugene O'Neill has earned himself a permanent niche in the history of the drama. As the winner of four Pulitzer prizes and one Nobel award, as a writer who even during his lifetime had achieved an international reputation, O'Neill at the very least commands our attention as an important figure in the history of modern drama. One critic has suggested that O'Neill is something of a prophet without honor in his own land, since the acclaim for O'Neill's work has generally been more enthusiastic abroad than it has been in America. Frederick I. Carpenter writes, "From the first Irishman who in 1923 rated him above Shaw and Synge, to the series of books about him in foreign languages published in the last two decades, he has been recognized even more as a major figure in world literature than as the leading American dramatist. Indeed, his world reputation has probably exceeded his American one from the time that his first plays became known. Much more than Lewis or Hemingway, who were chosen for the Nobel Prize primarily because of their American reputations, O'Neill has spoken directly to a world audience."

Two Reputations: It is not quite accurate, however, to suggest that O'Neill has not been honored by his own countrymen, for, in the words of John Gassner, "It is remarkable...that O'Neill should have won his reputation twice (once in the Twenties and once in the Fifties, after his death), without coming up to the literary standards of the day or winning the approbation of literary critics." Gassner goes on to suggest the sources of the continuing interest in O'Neill's plays: "There can be no doubt that O'Neill represented almost everything that is fundamentally modern about the American theater. He reflected also all that until recently was modern about the European theater in his restless experimentation, his avid cultivation of new ideas, his assertive individualism, and his intense unease. His success is that of a restless spirit honest enough to refuse to feel by rote, and his work is often as provocative as a leading question and as exciting (if also as precarious) as a plunge down a waterfall. His major defect is that he nearly always strains for **metaphysical** Angst, negativeness, and a sense of desolation not always well founded and more conducive to darkness than to light, liberation, and final purgation."

Admittedly Uneven: As the preceding quotation from Gassner indicates, even O'Neill's most ardent defenders have never denied the unevenness of his achievement. Joseph Wood Krutch, a long time O'Neill champion, in his American Drama Since 1918, makes this point in a general way when he says, "...The work of no other important contemporary has been more uneven. In the long list of his works are a number which were flat failures on the stage and at least a few which seem unfortunate from any standpoint. With the possible exception of one or two, even his best works nearly always succeed in embodying and that-possibly because the aim is so high-they are, in certain respects, less adequate to their purpose than the plays of lesser men." These words were written in 1939, before the publication or production of two major O'Neill plays, *The Iceman Cometh* (produced in 1946) and *Long Day's Journey into Night* (finished in 1940 but not produced until 1956). The same Mr. Krutch, without as yet being acquainted with O'Neill's later plays, suggested that the source of O'Neill's greatness lies in his attempts to translate his tragic sense of life into the idiom of the theater: "Mr. O'Neill is not, of course, our only playwright to attempt tragedy or near-tragedy. He is, however, the only one who has devoted himself consistently to the single task and hence the only one whom one thinks of as primarily a tragic writer." Doris Falk concludes her study of O'Neill by stressing the importance of the last plays in the dramatist's articulation of his tragic vision: "Whatever the verdict of posterity, there was something Promethean about this man who strove with defiant integrity to project through the drama his own vision of the truth. The scope of that vision-breadth and limitation, clarity and distortion-sprang from the inward agony of a mind doomed endlessly to feed upon itself. Inevitably that very torment which had given birth to the vision finally destroyed it. In the last plays O'Neill walked in the valley not of death alone, but of nothingness in which all values are illusions and all meaning fades before the terror of ambiguity………. His heroes…are doomed to assert their humanity by a struggle with ghosts in the dark night of the soul………. In the magnificent futility of the struggle is a fragment, at least, of the history of humanity."

Impact On American Theater: A recent critic of O'Neill, Edwin Engel, who has not been reluctant to point out the defects as well as the merits of the plays, has admirably summarized the significance of Eugene O'Neill for the history of the American theater. "O'Neill imparted to a large American audience an awareness of problems-psychological, philosophical, religious- with which the commercial theatre had never dared concern itself. He incited and inspired other playwrights with examples, good and bad, of dramaturgy by which to guide their course. He discomfited the multitude of hacks in the American theatre, thereby doing a significant service for the serious dramatist. Greater than the sum of its parts, his total achievement was an impressive triumph and made him, in an important sense, the master as well as the victim of the time." George Jean Nathan, a friend and early promoter of the playwright's (who was not averse to condemning what he regarded as the inferior plays), makes much the same point in mere flamboyant prose: "The American drama may still be very far from what one might desire it to be; but that in the last decade it has got much nearer to that desideratum than ever it got before must be obvious to anyone not wholly blind or British ….O'Neill alone and singlehanded waded through the dismal swamplands of American drama, bleak, squashy, and oozing sticky goo, and alone and singlehanded bore out of them the water lily that no American had found there before him."

Negative Critics: O'Neill, almost from the beginning of his career as a produced playwright, has not been without his detractors. These have included, among others, Bernard De Voto, Francis Fergusson, Eric Bentley, and Mary McCarthy. With the possible exception of a little regarded forty-eight-page pamphlet written by the playwright Virgil Geddes in 1934, probably the most vitriolic attack on O'Neill's work was Bernard De Voto's "minority report" published in *The Saturday Review* on the occasion of O'Neill's receiving the Nobel prize for literature in 1936. "Whatever his international reputation," wrote De Voto, "he can hardly be called an artist of the first rank; he is hardly even one of the first-rate figures of his own generation in America.... At best he is only the author of some extremely effective pieces for the theatre. At worst he has written some of the most pretentiously bad plays of our time. He has never been what the Guild and the Nobel jury unite in calling him, a great dramatist." O'Neill's plays, he continues, are a blend of "the novelties of the little theatre substituting for knowledge of the human heart, dodges and devices, a fortissimo assertion of significance, and a frantic grappling with what seem to be immensities but turn out to be one-syllable ideas and mostly wrong at that. The biggest wind-machine in our theatrical history is used to assist the enunciation of platitudes. Mr. O'Neill is dealing with ideas that elude him and straining for achievements beyond his power."

Bentleys' Judgments: Eric Bentley, in his influential and brilliantly stimulating work, *The Playwright as Thinker*, the book which established its author as the enfant terrible of American drama criticism, accused O'Neill of having sought greatness "by imitating and exploiting-the great, and he sees the permanence of art as a by-passing of the local and the temporal." Bentley further ascribes O'Neill's failure to his attempts to write tragedy in a time which has not been "ripe for tragedy." "O'Neill," says Bentley, "seems profound and turns out on further inspection to be silly.... Precisely because he pretends to too much, he attains too little. He is false, and he is false in a particularly unpleasant way." Returning some years later to the attack, Mr. Bentley, in a frequently reprinted essay, "Trying To Like O'Neill," tempered the severity of his judgments somewhat by paying more attention to O'Neill's strengths: "At one time he performed a historic function, that of helping the American theatre to grow up. In all his plays an earnest attempt is made to interpret life; this fact in itself places O'Neill above his predecessors in American drama and beside his colleagues in the novel and poetry. He was a good playwright insofar as he kept within the somewhat narrow range of his own sensibility. When he stays close to a fairly simple reality and when, by way of technique, he uses fairly simple forms of **realism** or fairly simple patterns of melodrama, he can render the bite and tang of reality or, alternatively, he can startle and stir us with his effects. If he is never quite a poet, he is occasionally able-as we have seen in *The Iceman*-to create the striking theatric image." Bentley concludes his attack on O'Neill with the interesting statement, "If one does not like O'Neill, it is not really he that one dislikes: it is our age-of which like the rest of us he is more the victim than the master."

O'Neill's Response To Criticism: O'Neill, like many artists before and after him, was often enraged by the attacks of critics. At least once, however, he rose above his sense of personal injury and took a larger view of the question. He once commented, according to George Jean Nathan, "I expect denunciation! It's generally sure to come. But I'm getting awfully callous to the braying, for or against. When they knock me, what the devil; they're really boosting me with their wholesale condemnations, for the reaction against such nonsense will come soon enough. These teapot turmoils at least keep me shaken up and convinced I'm on my way to something. I know enough history to realize that no one worth a damn ever escaped them-so it gives me hope. When I'm generally approved of, I begin to look in the mirror very skeptically and contemplate taking up some other career I might succeed at. So it's all tonic."

Gassner's Tribute: Perhaps a fitting conclusion to this attempt to survey the critical opinion of O'Neill's over-all achievement is a passage from John Gassner's tribute to the playwright who lay dying in a Boston hospital of an undiagnosable disease: "We men of the nineteen-twenties are not disposed to invalidate his rightful claim to being the only major dramatist of our theatre thus far. And we believe that the young generation would do well, too, if they drew closer to his work, not necessarily with reverence and awe but with the respectful attention that high purpose and intense wrestling with formidable demons or phantoms rather than with pigmies deserve. We may have a difficult time of it trying to convince the clever Eliot disciples. But surely, as T. S. Eliot himself can tell them, cleverness in art is not enough. There must be a real man with a real, if not always intellectually reducible, passion behind the art. O'Neill, we maintain, was such a man."

O'NEILL AS A CRAFTSMAN OF THE THEATER

Even the most negative of O'Neill's critics-including, as we have seen, De Voto and Bentley-have usually conceded, sometimes begrudgingly, the soundness of O'Neill's theatrical instincts and craftsmanship. The same Eric Bentley whose attempts to "like" O'Neill only succeeded in confirming him in his "dislike," admitted that "as a theatrical craftsman O'Neill is tremendously talented." And Bernard De Voto conceded that O'Neill "is… the author of some extremely effective pieces for the theater." Francis Fergusson, another unfriendly critic, condemned O'Neill for his melodrama and emotionalism, but also went on to say, "His naive belief in emotion is related to a priceless quality, which one may call the histrionic sincerity, the essence of mummery. Every dramatist as well as every actor depends for his power over his audience on his own belief in what he is trying to put on the stage, whether it be an emotion, a character, or a situation. An audience is extremely malleable. It may be swayed by suggestion, hypnotized by the concentration of the stage figure. This complete concentration, which would be wrecked by a wakeful critical faculty or a touch of humor at the wrong time, Mr. O'Neill possesses in a very high degree. It is the secret of his success; and when it is joined to an interest in a character, it produces his best scenes." T. S. Eliot is another one who paid tribute to the power of O'Neill's plays in the theater. "I realize," wrote Eliot, "that a play must be judged from seeing it on the stage as well as from reading the text. This is particularly true, I think, of the plays of Eugene O'Neill. It is only within the last two or three years that I have seen plays by him performed.... I should like to say that I place his work very high indeed." And in the words of Harold Clurman, "It is indisputable that O'Neill's plays are nearly always more impressive on the stage than on the printed page."

Naturally enough, the O'Neill admirers have not been blind to the immense theatrical skills which this actor's son brought to the creation of his plays. The praise of Alan S. Downer in a *Theatre Arts* article written in 1951 may be taken as typical of this critical recognition. Downer writes, "Other men have conceived tragic situations, and other men have made full use of the resources of the modern stage. Few, however, have achieved a balanced combination of the two with the consistency of Eugene O'Neill. O'Neill has a unique combination of skill and vision: born and raised in the theatre he was well-versed in the secrets of stage effect; years of travel and experience gave him a sense of the mystery of life which prevented him from using his skill for effect alone…. The use of the material of the theatre, settings and make-up and action, on several levels achieves an effect similar to the effect of poetic language in the older drama, and accounts for the impact of much of O'Neill's work, in spite of the lack of poetic language in his dialogue." This substitution of the poetry of the theater for conventional dramatic poetry is also cited by John Gassner, who writes, "Those who press the charge of want of 'poetry' in the man should be reminded, moreover, that he got his 'poetry,' as other modern playwrights have done, not from verbal beauty but from the breadth and reach of his imagination, mood, or feeling, and especially, from his theatrical - at times exaggeratedly theatrical - sense. If he was not felicitous in creating verbal poetry, he often created a 'poetry of the theatre.'"

THE LANGUAGE OF O'NEILL'S PLAYS

O'Neill's lack of verbal felicity, hinted at in the passages just quoted from Downer and Gassner, has been the most frequently repeated and in fact the most serious charge leveled against O'Neill's artistry. Few, including the dramatist himself, have denied O'Neill's vulnerability in this area. O'Neill made claims for himself-some would say pretentious claims - as a poet. In a letter to Arthur Hobson Quinn he wrote, "Where I feel myself most neglected is just where I set most store by myself - as a bit of a poet, who has labored with the spoken word to evolve original rhythms of beauty, where beauty apparently isn't...and to see the transfiguring nobility of tragedy, in as near the Greek sense as one can grasp it, in seemingly the most ignoble, debased lives." In another letter to the same Professor Quinn, however, O'Neill admitted with a mixture of disarming candor and question-begging rationalization, "I haven't got [great language]. And, by way of self-consolation, I don't think, from the evidence of all that is being written today, that great language is possible for anyone living in the discordant, broken, faithless rhythm of our time. The best one can do is to be pathetically eloquent by one's moving, dramatic in articulations." Leaving aside the questionable assumptions underlying O'Neill's explanations of his stylistic inadequacies, one cannot help being impressed by that quality which probably more than any other stamped the man and his work: his honesty, his authenticity. It is interesting to observe, furthermore, how closely O'Neill's analysis of the reasons for his failures approximate those of one of his most severe critics. Eric Bentley, it will be remembered, was inclined to blame O'Neill's weaknesses less on the man than on the age which produced him.

A Weakness Admitted By All: From friend and foe alike, the indictments of O'Neill's awkward use of language have a familiar, almost monotonous ring to them. Krutch writes, "For all that he is so prolific, he has no facility; there is a continual, seldom wholly successful struggle, not only with the central conception but even with the language itself, so that one often gets the impression of positive clumsiness, as though neither the imagination nor the tongue was quite articulate enough to achieve full or clear expression." Edmund Wilson puts it more briefly: "As a rule the plays of O'Neill are singularly uninviting on the printed page. The dialogue is raw and prosaic, in texture quite undistinguished." Mary McCarthy, reviewing *The Iceman Cometh* in 1946 in *Partisan Review*, is predictably more waspish in her condemnation: "O'Neill belongs to that group of American authors, which includes Farrell and Dreiser, whose choice of vocation was a kind of triumphant **catastrophe**; none of these men possessed the slightest ear for the word, the sentence, the speech, the paragraph; all of them, however, have, so to speak, enforced the career they decreed for themselves by a relentless policing of their beat. What they produce is hard to praise or to condemn; how is one to judge the great, logical symphony of a tone-deaf musician?" Edwin Engel's tone is a bit less harsh, but the final judgment is no less severe than Miss McCarthy's; "O'Neill's style remained not only strained and turgid, but awkward, inarticulate, banal." John Gassner, as usual, strikes a more balanced note in his appraisal of O'Neill's language: "If he was not felicitous in creating verbal poetry, he often created a 'poetry of the theatre.'"

O'NEILL'S RELIGIOUS VIEWS

Certainly one of the major sources of O'Neill's claims upon our attention is the largeness of the subjects he chose to deal with, the profundity of the questions he chose to probe in his plays. As he himself once wrote, "To me, the tragic alone has that significant beauty which is truth. It is the meaning of life - and the hope." At another time he remarked "Most modern plays are concerned with the relation between man and man, but that does not interest me at all. I am interested only in the relation between man and God." Commenting on the breadth and scope of O'Neill's artistic aims, Lionel Trilling, a major voice in American literary criticism, wrote, "Not only has O'Neill tried to encompass more of life than most American writers of his time but, almost alone among them, he has persistently tried to solve it. When we understand this we understand that his stage devices are not fortuitous technique; his masks and abstractions, his double personalities, his drum beats and engine rhythms are the integral and necessary expression of his temper of mind and the task it set itself." In more specific terms Doris Falk described the tragic dimension of O'Neill's plays as follows: "O'Neill thought of himself as a writer of 'ironic tragedy,' but **irony** requires a detachment which he found impossible. Pity, indignation, despair at the human position, robbed his tragedies of the irony he intended them to convey. The sneer became only the protective mask of a face distorted by suffering; the ironic words were drowned in cries of anguish. The plays are attempts to explain human suffering and, somehow, to justify it. The result is not **irony**, but the classic twofold justification of the ways of God-or fate-to man: first, that suffering and the very need to explain and symbolize it are the fountainhead of human action and creativity; and second, that fated though he may be, man is ultimately a free and responsible agent who brings most of his grief upon himself through pride."

O'Neill's World A "Bestiary": Writing behind the cloak of anonymity provided by the *London Times Literary Supplement*, a faceless critic sneeringly dismissed O'Neill's attempts to illuminate the big questions by referring to the playwright's philosophy and then questioning whether "philosophy is a word which is applicable to the mass of undisciplined emotions and jejune opinions which appear in his plays." The same critic continues, "The most obvious difference between Aeschylus, Shakespeare, and Mr. O'Neill is that the two former loved mankind, but the last feels only contemptuous pity for it. The strongest passion animating his characters is hate.... There is no sign of nobility in the characters who populate his plays. Not one of them has been made in the image of God. All of them bear the mark of the beast. The best of them are only negatively good, inertly abstaining from evil as if they were less in love with virtue than terrified of vice. Wandering through his underworld, and holding our noses as we wander, we have difficulty in believing that even it could have existed without one positively good and likable inhabitant." This nameless critic with the hypersensitive olfactory nerves concludes this section of his diatribe by condemning the world O'Neill created in his plays as "a bestiary full of vulpine animals and crushed worms." One possible response to such gratuitously violent abuse is to quote the remark with which O'Neill concluded an article he wrote for the *New York Tribune* in 1921: "Damn the optimists anyway! They make life so darned hopeless!"

On one point all are agreed: Eugne O'Neill aimed high. The differences of opinion arise over the question concerning how successfully O'Neill translated his aims into viable artistic terms.

O'NEILL AS A SOCIAL CRITIC

It is always a dangerously misleading exercise to look upon literary works of art as so many sociological documents. At the same time, however, it must be said that a play, for example, stands in some relationship to the social matrix in which it was formed. This relationship varies from writer to writer and from work to work, and the bond between the literary artifact and the social context may be that of a reflection, a commentary, or a shaper of the social milieu, or some combination of all three. An O'Casey or a Brecht, for example, have frequently in their plays used the stage as a forum for direct comment upon the political and social questions of the day. To a lesser extent and in a more oblique fashion this is also true of Eugene O'Neill, even though the topical immediacy of his plays is less apparent than in the works of other playwrights. This remains true despite O'Neill's own disclaimer of any social or political purpose in his plays. In an interview in 1922 with Oliver M. Sayler, O'Neill remarked, "... As we progress, we are always seeing further than we can reach. I suppose that is one reason why I have come to feel so indifferent toward political and social movements of all kinds. Time was when I was an active socialist, and, after that, a philosophical anarchist. But today I can't feel that anything like that really matters. It is rather amusing to me to see how seriously some people take politics and social questions and how much they expect of them. Life as a whole is changed very little, if at all, as a result of their course." And a quarter of a century later, during the rehearsals of *The Iceman Cometh*, an actor questioned the dramatist concerning his views on the labor movement. "I am a philosophical anarchist," O'Neill replied, "which means, 'Go to it, but leave me out of it'."

Emphasis On Inner Conflict: There is no question, of course, that O'Neill's brooding introspection, his agonizing wrestling with his family, his God, and his own tormented self, tended to produce an emphasis in his plays upon the inner struggles of his characters with themselves and with each other, rather than with their environment. A writer, nevertheless, cannot escape his own values and the judgments flowing from those values which are inevitably woven into the texture of his work. We have already seen, for example, that Sam Evans in *Strange Interlude* embodies to some extent the dramatist's negative views on the American business ethos. The emphasis, however, is always upon the internal conflict, even in those plays which deal with a pressing social problem, such as, for example, *The Hairy Ape* (the class struggle), and *All God's Chillun Got Wings* (race).

O'Neill's concern with "the condition of the individual soul" represented for one critic a retreat from the vital area of social concern. In her book *American Playwrights: 1918–1938: The Theatre Retreats from Reality*, Eleanor Flexner criticized O'Neill for his lack of social consciousness. Her book was published, significantly, in 1938, during the decade when social awareness was the overriding concern of America's writers. Doris Alexander, in her article "O'Neill As Social Critic" concludes her analysis with this judgment: "The main trend in Eugene O'Neill's social criticism is negative. He condemns the capitalist state, but sees no hope for man in any other kind of a state. Whatever hope he sees for man lies in individuals who may have the courage to possess their own souls…. Ultimately,

Eugene O'Neill's social criticism cancels itself out, for he not only condemns all of society as is, he rejects all solutions for making it something better. He accepts no answer to life, but death." John Gassner, however, takes a somewhat different view: "O'Neill, who contributed to the Socialist Call in his early days of journalism and who mingled with the political vanguard of liberals associated with the Provincetown Players, was a social critic of sorts.... O'Neill was not unaware of society and its effects...although neither his anti-political nor his leftist critics have cared to concede this fact.... He depicted environment scrupulously. And he was virtually the first serious American dramatist of any standing to bring characters from all walks of life on to the stage, noting their origins of race and background with sympathy and understanding. It would not be difficult to sustain the point that he gave us social pictures and socially-conditioned, if not altogether socially-determined, actions with greater credibility and vitality than most 'social dramatists' of the nineteen-thirties and since then." It must be admitted, however, that O'Neill's naturalistically accurate rendering of sociological detail and his attempts to capture the rhythms of authentic American idiom and dialect hardly make him a social critic. Whatever social commentary there is in the plays is there incidentally or implicitly. Lionel Trilling perhaps comes closer to a true appraisal of O'Neill's attitude toward society. "For O'Neill," Trilling writes, "since as far back as *The Hairy Ape*, there has been only the individual and the universe. The social organism has meant nothing." Several of O'Neill's own comments on different occasions would tend to reinforce Mr. Trilling's judgment. In a letter to Barrett Clark, for instance, O'Neill wrote, "Noting the way the world wags, I am sure that Man has definitely decided to destroy himself, and this seems to be the only truly wise decision he has ever made." And in a press conference in 1946 he made much the same point in even more nihilistic terms: "If the human race is so damned stupid that in two thousand years it hasn't had brains enough to appreciate that the secret of happiness is contained in one simple sentence which you'd think any grammar school kid could understand and apply, then it's time we dumped it down the nearest drain and let the ants have a chance."

O'NEILL'S INTEREST IN PSYCHOLOGY

If O'Neill's plays have on the whole tended to ignore the immediate political and social issues of the day, they have conversely tended to turn in upon man's psychic life. The play that we have been focusing upon in this study is an outstanding example of O'Neill's interest in the psychological life of his characters. He himself described *Strange Interlude* as "an attempt at the new masked psychological drama...without masks." Oscar Cargill remarked concerning O'Neill's interest in psychology: "O'Neill's interest in depth psychology is important only insofar as it helped him to write effective dramas. Much Freudianism and Jungianism was attributed to him by critics who, in our Freudian age, have learned to look at people and literature from a psychoanalytic point of view. O'Neill himself disclaimed any 'conscious use of psychoanalytical material,' although he admitted having read two books by Freud and two by Jung, and we know that he underwent psychoanalysis in 1927."

Jung And The Freudians: Doris Falk, whose study is mainly concerned with the psychological aspects of O'Neill's plays, stresses O'Neill's affinities with Jung: "Jung sees man's primary need not in the desire to satisfy physical drives or to fulfill any single emotional necessity such as power, security, or love, but in a longing for a life of meaning and purpose-for a sense of order in the universe to which man can belong and in which he can trust. Jung is a mystic in the same sense that

O'Neill is mystical: He recognizes what he calls 'psychological truth' as existing independently of objectively provable fact.... O'Neill assumes, with Jung, that one's problems and actions spring not only from his personal unconscious mind, but from a 'collective unconscious' shared by the race as a whole, manifesting itself in archetypal symbols and patterns latent in the minds of all men." Miss Falk further points out the ties between many of O'Neill's insights and the work of later writers on psychoanalysis: "If O'Neill has consciously echoed some of the thought of Jung, he has unconsciously anticipated the findings of the 'Neo-Freudians,' Karen Horney and Erich Fromm.... The work of the Neo-Freudians, whether or not theirs is the most effective school of modern psychology, both reflects and illuminates the patterns of human behavior which O'Neill described from his own observation and experience. These same patterns are described with varying terminologies in all the major psychoanalytic systems, especially in those of Jung and Adler. The Neo-Freudians, however, particularly Horney, have provided a theory which gives order and coherence to O'Neill's unconscious self-revelations and clearly relates them to his conscious philosophy." The same author points out the significance of O'Neill's psychological interests for his dramatic purposes: "At the core of O'Neill's work is his conception of the inward, uniquely personal experience of modern man. Upon the playwright, then, rests the burden of convincing his audience that his heroes, himself, and they are one."

Psychological Gas: Eric Bentley, probably the most articulate and influential of the anti-O'Neill critics, has found O'Neill's use of psychoanalytical theory to be one of the most objectionable features of the plays. After accusing O'Neill of inflating his plays with "psychological gas," Bentley continues, "O'Neill has boasted his ignorance of Freud but such ignorance is not enough. He should be ignorant also of the watered-down Freudianism of

Sardi's [a New York restaurant where theatrical people gather] and the Algonquin [a New York hotel where certain literary figures have been known to congregate], the Freudianism of all those who are ignorant of Freud, the Freudianism of the subintelligentsia."

As is the case, then, with just about every aspect of O'Neill's plays, there is a wide divergence of critical opinion as to the success with which the playwright has incorporated the findings of modern psychology into his work.

CRITICAL OPINION ON STRANGE INTERLUDE

Probably the outstanding example of Eugene O'Neill's wholesale use of modern psychology in one of his plays is the work under examination in this study, *Strange Interlude*. The critic Oscar Cargill has condemned the play roundly precisely for the heavy doses of neo-Freudianism which O'Neill has injected into the play. "If ever a play were designed," wrote Cargill, "to tickle the bourgeois palate, this one was…. *Strange Interlude* is not an original dramatic composition, but a case history." Mr. Bentley, predictably, found fault with what he regarded as the psychological shallowness of this work: "A hundred novelists have dealt more subtly with hidden motives than O'Neill did in his famous essay in psychological subtlety, *Strange Interlude*, a play which is equally inferior as a study of upper-class Americans." But here again O'Neill has had his defenders. Kenneth MacGowan described *Strange Interlude* as a play in which "he gave us the outward, realistic aspects of his people and the outward realistic talk that they would use. Then, between almost every pair of speeches, he dug down into the minds of his characters and brought out their thoughts in speech that the audience, but not the other characters, could hear. This device was more than soliloquy and it did more than expose the thoughts of people. It was a living and exciting dialogue of a new kind. To the dramatic contrasts and conflicts of ordinary spoken dialogue O'Neill added the contrasts and conflicts of thought. There was the speech of Nina against the speech of Charlie, the thought of Nina against the speech of Nina, the thought of Nina against the thought of Charlie, and sometimes the speech of one against the thought of the other. It is this new dramatic contrast that sets off O'Neill's method from the free soliloquy and asides of the older romantic stage. And it is the consistent use of this contrast through a complete evening that takes O'Neill's device out of the class of any of its recent forerunners."

Critical Opinion Divided: Aside from the critical arguments over the psychologizing in *Strange Interlude* - a question which is, of course, central to any discussion of the play - the lines of opinion are about as evenly and as sharply divided here as on any other question concerning O'Neill's plays. The critical reviews of the 1928 production struck the discordant notes which have been resounding ever since. Although notices of plays written by daily reviewers tend to be hastily written, unreflective, ephemeral reports of a theatrical event rather than thoughtful criticism, still these early reviews suggest the lines which future criticism of this play tended to follow. Dudley Nichols, reviewing the play for *the World*, wrote, "The Theatre Guild produced Eugene O'Neill's *Strange Interlude* last night and it needs all the restraint a reporter can muster not to stamp the occasion, without a second thought, the most important event in the present era of the American theatre.... The most that can be said for the play is that when the 900 persons went with illuminated faces out of the small John Golden Theatre at the later hour their faces registered tiredness but not boredom, weariness but not ennui. It was the honest fatigue of people who have shared profound emotional experiences." The critic for the Sun was equally enthusiastic: "*Strange Interlude* stands firm and giant-sized as a giver of new scopes, as a hewer of ways for such truths as the usual drama can scarce imply, as a method to meet the need, today's immense need, for plays that can ably cope with Freud. If only for that reason - and I guarantee to find you others - it is the most significant contribution any American has made to the stage." Brooks Atkinson, writing in the *Times*, praised the play sparingly and then characterized the asides as "nickel-weekly jargon…offered as thinking…. What fresh light do they reflect upon character? What do they express which cannot be conveyed vividly through the silent instrument of acting? What, in fine, distinguishes *Strange Interlude* from the old three-decker novel?" But another critic praised the asides: "…*Strange Interlude* is not a play for lazy drama lovers. His unlimited employment of 'asides' to describe the unspoken thoughts of his characters is more of a whip than a cushion to our imagination, and it keeps us busy…." Robert Benchley in *The New Yorker*, on the other hand, criticized the play as overwritten: "In proposing to give voice to the thoughts of his characters, Mr. O'Neill lays himself open to comparison with James Joyce, Virginia Woolf, and the other stream-of-consciousness novelists. It is a comparison he can ill support. The turbulent stream of consciousness Joyce photographs so perfectly finds itself, in *Strange Interlude*, confined to neat concrete containers which are far more like summaries of the momentary situation as Mr. O'Neill wishes one to understand it than like what the characters are actually thinking at the time. They create the impression that Mr. O'Neill has done the groundwork which every dramatist must do, so much to his own satisfaction that he hasn't been able to rub any of it out, or that, unwilling to trust anything to his actors, he is trying to do their work for them too." Joseph Wood Krutch, who was, as we have seen, an O'Neill champion - with some reservations-reviewed *Strange Interlude* for *The Nation* and decided that the play "does give something - some depth, some solidity - which no play has ever had, and its strange method does make possible a kind of virtue new to dramatic art.... It can only be said...that *Strange Interlude* conquers a new province for the theatre. In the past our dramatists have been lazily content to say that most of the things which gave modern literature its excuse for being were 'not suited to the stage.' Mr. O'Neill has succeeded in making them dramatic." Writing a few years later about this play, the same critic in his *The American Drama Since 1918* tempered his enthusiasm somewhat: "The central situation of the play is powerfully imagined and, despite a certain inconclusiveness, it is continuously absorbing - at least up to the last section, after the beginning of which it becomes more and more apparent that the piece will end without ever achieving any satisfactory clarification of all that has been suggested. But the interest is rather interest in a static situation than in a developing drama. What we feel most powerfully is the mood generated by the spectacle of this group of people, each caught between the horns of his particular psychological dilemma, and each foredoomed from the beginning to struggles which are bound to be ineffectual.... The actual events of the play seem usually of secondary interest, sometimes even arbitrary or fortuitous. Because the characters themselves do not believe anything, they cannot really want anything. The life of each is over before the play begins and they fight sham battles over issues which might be decided either one way or the other without changing the fact that all concerned are already damned." And, finally, Edwin Engel tends to locate the faults of the play in the failure of O'Neill's style: "The faults of *Strange Interlude* stem neither from its innovations nor from a failure to be dramatic. Its faults are those that have inhered in many of O'Neill's plays: a rhetorical and turgid style; an intensity of feeling 'that is in excess of the facts'; a content that is frequently closer to bathos than to tragedy."

Conclusion: And so the argument goes on, over *Strange Interlude*, over O'Neill in general. In many ways this oversized play can stand as a microcosmic version of the problems that O'Neill's poses for criticism, for here are his strengths and his weaknesses, nakedly paraded for all to see. Out of the dialectical clash of critical opinion which attends any discussion of an O'Neill play, one can hopefully expect an eventual sharpening of insight, a deepening of judgment, a raising of taste. Eugene O'Neill was, if nothing else, a catalytic force in the creative and critical life of the American theater. For this at least we must be grateful. We must be grateful too for the shining example of literary integrity which O'Neill's dramatic career represents. And finally we must be grateful to the lonely man who has left to posterity a legacy of theatrical writing which, it seems safe to say, contains at least some work which will satisfy the highest dramatic standards and give pleasure to the most divergent types of literary palate. One suspects that O'Neill's place in the history of world drama will not be a modest one.

STRANGE INTERLUDE

ESSAY QUESTIONS AND ANSWERS

Question: Discuss O'Neill's use of technical innovations in *Strange Interlude*.

Answer: Like August Strindberg, the great Swedish play-wright he had chosen as his literary mentor, Eugene O'Neill refused to be satisfied with the surface **realism** which has been the stock in trade of so much serious modern drama since Ibsen. It remains true, however, that the vast majority of modern playwrights - including Ibsen himself - sooner or later broke out of the restricting confines of the realistic play with its box set, naturalistic furnishings, middle-class milieu, its attempts to simulate the speech of everyday life, its general striving after photographic accuracy.

New Freedom: Historically, the introduction of **realism** into the theater and its brilliant exploitation by such masters as Ibsen and Chekhov liberated the drama from the stale **conventions** of romantic, sentimental theater, from the artificial, synthetic, machine-like neatness of the "well-made play," from the moral and social tracts thinly disguised as plays - the pieces a these or thesis plays which were particularly popular in nineteenth-century

France. The new freedom to discuss openly and candidly many of the ideas and problems which were keeping nineteenth-century Europe in a ferment helped to make the theater immediately relevant to the life of the age. The **conventions** of **realism** originally represented an opening of windows on the stale playhouses of Europe; the new **realism** challenged the imagination and the social conscience of such revolutionary artists as Ibsen, Hauptmann, Shaw, Chekhov, Gorki, Strindberg, and O'Casey.

New Confinement: This same new dramatic **realism**, however, soon revealed itself, in its concern with the flatness and banalities of everyday existence, as a confining halter on the dramatic imagination. Right from the start, consequently, the leading dramatists of Europe found themselves in revolt against **realism** - sometimes partially, sometimes completely. Art, after all, is not photography. The work of art which most closely approximates the conditions of everyday life is not necessarily the greater part for its photographic precision of detail. A great part of the history of modern drama, consequently, can be charted in terms of the modern playwright's willingness to avail himself of the new freedom which was realism's legacy, without, however, confining himself to all the limitations of the "fourth wall." The rebellion against **realism** - or realism striving to escape or transcend itself - is in one form or another the story of modern drama from Henrik Ibsen to Bertolt Brecht. The works of Eugene O'Neill are no exception to this formula, even though O'Neill's straining to burst the bonds of theatrical **realism** took forms which were as individual, as unique, as the man himself.

O'Neill's Revolt: It is important to view O'Neill's plays in general and *Strange Interlude* in particular against this historical background of the adoption of and revolt against dramatic **realism**. O'Neill was not, as we have seen, alone in his impatience with the straight realistic play. His restless spirit, always struggling with the medium of his art, always attempting to find new ways of embodying dramatically those things he wanted to say, those questions he wanted to raise, drove him into various kinds of experimentation, ranging from the naturalism of his early sea plays to the expressionism of *The Hairy Ape*, *The Emperor Jones*, and *Lazarus Laughed*. It is in the context of O'Neill's refusal to remain satisfied with established dramatic forms that we should examine his technical pioneering in *Strange Interlude*.

Unconventional Length: The first fact which strikes one about this play is its great length. *Strange Interlude* is not, of course, O'Neill's only long play. It is interesting that the playwright who launched his career on a flood of one-acters soon became enamored of the long play. *Marco Millions* was originally two plays; *Mourning Becomes Electra*, with its thirty-seven scenes, is a huge, sprawling attempt to write a Greek trilogy in modern dress; *The Iceman Cometh*, and *Long Day's Journey into Night*, two of his last and greatest plays, are considerably longer than average; and at his death he left unfinished an eleven-part dramatic cycle of **epic** proportions. It is obvious that O'Neill felt hampered, in trying to search in depth and at length the meaning of his characters' lives, by the traditional two- to two-and-a-half-hour long play. It is not that O'Neill was incapable of packing his dramatic ideas into the smaller vehicle. *The Emperor Jones* and *The Hairy Ape*, to mention only two works, attest to his ability to write successful shorter plays. It was more a question of the playwright's striving for the spaciousness and leisure which provided the novelist with the time and opportunity to probe the large questions of human existence through a careful and prolonged study of his characters and their mutual interactions. Just as Zola, Proust, Joyce, and Mann (not to mention the Victorians with their "triple-decker" novels) were expanding the limits of the novel in an attempt to embody in fiction the social and psychological fullness of life, so too Eugene O'Neill was attempting to incorporate some of the same artistic breadth into the traditionally briefer, more concise dramatic form. *Strange Interlude*, consequently, brings its audience into the theater at five-thirty, releases them for an eighty-minute dinner intermission, and sends them home after eleven o'clock. In the meantime the spectators have been invited to share, not in the narration of events (which is the novelist's method), but in the representation of an action, which is, after all, the definition of a play. To depict the major **episodes** in Nina Leeds' struggle for happiness with the fullness he felt the subject demanded, O'Neill felt he needed no less than some five hours. It is not so much that O'Neill was garrulous and long-winded - though he sometimes is, often deliberately so. He simply asserted the artist's right to make demands upon his audience. No fair-minded person can say, a priori, that length in and of itself is either good or bad. Each work must be judged on its own terms, and while there are those who would dismiss *Strange Interlude* as an inflated piece of dramaturgy, the play still has its stalwart champions. If we are to believe contemporary accounts of the play's first production in 1928, the audiences left the theater exhausted but deeply moved.

Asides And Soliloquies: The second major innovation in *Strange Interlude*, closely related to what was discussed above, is the extended use of asides and soliloquies. The aside and the soliloquy are, of course, **conventions** as old as the theater itself, as every reader of Greek and Elizabethan drama well knows. What is novel about these **conventions** in *Strange Interlude* is the extent to which the playwright made use of them. The extraordinary length of the play is largely the result of the extended use of the soliloquy and the aside.

In a play whose form is basically realistic, the inclusion of this **convention** allows the playwright a greater flexibility and scope in bringing to the surface the inner flow of thoughts, desires, and responses which so often differ dramatically from the external words and gestures of the characters. In addition to providing fullness and depth to the characters, this device also serves to thicken the tensions and conflicts of the play and to increase the opportunities for dramatic **irony**. The struggles in this play are as often as not the struggles of the characters against themselves as much as against other people and circumstances.

Impact Of Psychology: The impact of modern psychology was first beginning to make itself felt on a wide scale during the decade of the twenties, and the comparison of the human mind to an iceberg, nine-tenths of which is hidden beneath the surface, is an idea which psychological research had begun to make generally available. The relationship between this psychological truth and O'Neill's interest in the inner, "unspoken" thoughts of his characters is obvious. The revelation of the characters' conflicts with their own drives, impulses, and yearnings, their attempts to suppress their inner selves, form an important part of the dramatic texture of this play. Certain novelists had been utilizing the interior monologue in their works before O'Neill wrote *Strange Interlude*, and it is probable that, in his general attempts to emulate the writers of fiction in this play, he was influenced by the example of such artists as James Joyce and Virginia Woolf.

One of O'Neill's friendly critics and early admirers, Barrett Clark, has found fault with what he considers the excessive use of asides in this play. Although he bestows praise in general on *Strange Interlude*, Clark raises serious questions about O'Neill's skill in the employment of this device. "Is it always necessary," he asks, "to express aloud what one thinks and feels? Cannot the actor occasionally show it? I believe that perhaps one-third of all the words not intended to be heard by the other characters might have been omitted without the loss of anything essential. O'Neill has overworked his device." Apparently even those willing to applaud O'Neill for his artistic experimentation feel, at least on occasion, that they have had too much of a good thing.

Question: What is the significance of the title, *Strange Interlude*?

Answer: A key to the significance of the play's title is provided in more than one place. As the surviving major characters begin settling down to the twilight oblivion of a loveless old age, Charles Marsden comments to himself, "Age's terms of peace, after the long interlude of war with life, have still to be concluded." And toward the end of this final act he says to Nina, "There was something unreal in all that happened since you first met Gordon Shaw.... So let's you and me forget the whole distressing episode, regard it as an interlude of trial and preparation, say, in which our souls have been scraped clean of impure flesh and made worthy to bleach in peace." And Nina, wearing "a strange smile," replies, "Strange interlude! Yes, our lives are merely strange dark interludes in the electrical display of God the Father!"

The phrase from which the play takes its title, then, has become a **metaphor** for, and a comment on, the pitifully futile struggles enacted by human beings before a careless, indifferent God. The term interlude signifies something which comes between, and in this case it is Nina Leeds' strange or meaningless quest to achieve happiness, a quest which is the interval between the quiet, peaceful periods on either side of the interval. From the time of her entrance into womanhood, that is, the time of her sexual awakening as a woman, until her withdrawal from the arena into the sexually neutral arms of Charles Marsden, Nina's life - or interlude - is one long round of agitated, unsuccessful groping. She herself in the last act looks back yearningly at her early youth, "before I fell in love with Gordon Shaw and all this tangled mess of love and hate and pain and birth began!" Insofar as *Strange Interlude* can be looked upon as a dramatic **metaphor** for Eugene O'Neill's vision of life, then to that extent can one speak of this vision as dark, morose, pessimistic, and, perhaps, tragic. Such a view is succinctly suggested by the title of this play.

Question: In what sense can Nina Leeds be described as a modern Everywoman?

Answer: At one stage during the writing of *Strange Interlude*, O'Neill, writing to a friend, referred to it as his "woman play." The phrase provides a hint as to how the **protagonist** of this play might be regarded, but even if we had only the evidence of the text itself (actually the only valid evidence anyway), it becomes clear that Nina Leeds is one of the truly large figures of the modern stage. When one compares her to some of the other great heroines of modern dramatic literature - Ibsen's Rebecca West, Solveig, and Hedda Gabler, Strindberg's Miss Julie, Shaw's St. Joan, O'Casey's Juno Boyle, Anouilh's Antigone, Williams' Blanche Dubois - Nina Leeds seems to stand apart, to possess some peculiar qualities uniquely her own. A moment's reflection suggests that throughout the twenty-eight-year interlude covered by the play she has played more different kinds of "woman roles" than probably any other figure in theatrical history. The ultimate **irony**, of course, is that her passing from one role to another fails to provide her with the fulfillment, the sense of identity, the happiness, she so desperately seeks.

Comparison With Other Heroines: It is not that Nina Leeds is necessarily a greater creation than any of the figures of modern drama mentioned above. She is not really any more neurotically driven than Miss Julie or Blanche DuBois. (The attempt to scale or "place" neuroses or to compare neurotic personalities is, in any case, a dubious practice at best.) Nina cannot be described as more destructive than Rebecca West or Hedda Gabler; neither does she have the single-minded toughness of a St. Joan or an Antigone. She possesses none of the redemptive love of Solveig in Ibsen's Peer Gynt. She has none of the firmness or the earth-rooted heroism of Juno Boyle. And yet it can be argued that in some ways O'Neill's heroine transcends these others, if in no other way, at least in terms of the sheer quantity of feminine functions she attempts to fulfill. As the young daughter of a New England widower, a professor of classics, she is the embodiment of genteel, middle-class respectability: civilized, sensitive, repressed. Her life seemed at first to have been following the prescribed, classical lines of the American myth: wholesome, attractive young co-ed from a "good" home falls in love with and is about to marry the all-American dream boy - the handsome, popular, successful college hero, Gordon Shaw. The traditional, expected course of events - church wedding followed by a dignified lawn reception followed by a European honeymoon followed by a discreet number of children and the comfortable life of a cultivated woman contentedly married to a successful business scion - this course of events is rudely interrupted by the cruel quirks of a mysterious, hostile fate. World War One erupts, Gordon becomes a pilot, is dissuaded by Nina's father from marrying her until after the war, and is shot down in flames two days before the armistice.

Human Choices: It should be noted that Nina's enactment of the great American love myth is thwarted not merely by external, impersonal forces over which she has no control. The destruction of Nina's dream castle is as much the result of certain more or less freely made human decisions as it is the result of a cruelly impersonal destiny. For one thing Professor Leeds interferes in the lives of his daughter and her fiancé, thereby thwarting a marriage which, Nina later reflects, would at least have provided her empty life with something: an ephemeral moment of happiness, a memory, possibly even a child. Gordon, responding to the professor's appeal to his honor, decides not to marry the girl he loves. Nina - and this is extremely important as the choice which triggered her own inner, gnawing guilt - refused to submit sexually to her lover before his departure. The memory of this refusal haunts Nina, creates deep-seated anxieties, drives her to a number of experiments, and attempts to allay her feelings of guilt, and in the final analysis prevents her entering into any kind of mature love relationship with another human being.

Wide Range Of Experiences: Deprived of her lover and husband-to-be by his ironically cruel death, Nina rejects her father, engages in a number of promiscuous affairs with wounded soldiers, marries a simple-minded young man who worships her from afar as some kind of a goddess, forms an adulterous liaison with the attractive young doctor who had helped to arrange her marriage, bears a child by him, smotheringly attempts to possess this new love object, loses him in marriage to a "rival," finally marries an older, sexless father figure, and wearily settles down to a twilight, passionless existence. This represents, it must be admitted, quite a spectrum of experiences for one woman to undergo, either in life or within the confines of one play. Molly Bloom, the earth-goddess figure of James Joyce's Ulysses, has little on Nina Leeds, at least in terms of the sheer range of womanly experiences each lives through. Comparisons are admittedly not only odious, but dangerous as well. There is no attempt here to suggest that O'Neill has achieved anything like the quintessential modern woman attempted by Joyce. Since the two men, furthermore, worked in different artistic media, any large-scale comparison is automatically excluded. Joyce's **epic** heroine is mentioned here only to suggest a possible frame of reference for discussion.

The dramatic **climax** of Nina Leeds' attempts to become a full woman by simultaneously playing many roles and by manipulating male objects is achieved in the powerful curtain scene which ends Act Six. Surrounded by her three servile men - Marsden (father figure), Evans (the husband), Darrell (the lover) - reminiscing about the dead Gordon, who, she thinks, mystically returned from the dead to impregnate her, and musing fondly about her infant son sleeping upstairs, Nina Leeds is at the zenith of her strange journey. Her triumph, however, is as short-lived as it is hollow. The serenity of the tableau-like scene which ends Act Six is more apparent than real, since it is not built on love. Nina, whose psychic wounds have made her incapable of love, is self-destructively driven to possess and dominate her men. The final three acts of the play chart the inevitable dissolution of the pseudo-relationships Nina has established as substitutes for love.

Nina's Roles: Daughter, fiancée, whore, bride, adulteress, mother, and finally child once more - these are the lives Nina leads, the masks she wears, the roles she plays. Observing the wide range of female identities Nina successively adopts and sheds, one is, it would seem, justified in describing her as a modern Everywoman. In the words of Edwin Engel, the critic who first applied the phrase to O'Neill's heroine, "In *Strange Interlude* he is concerned with the anguish of everywoman." Further elaborating the point in another place, Engel writes, "A realistic play, Interlude exemplifies that 'special sort of naturalism which develops into the mythical.' The pagan myth has been abandoned; the new myth is more permeated by the psychological tendency." Barrett Clark, in his study *Eugene O'Neill, The Man and His Plays*, feels that in striving to create this modern Everywoman, the dramatist has sacrificed psychological plausibility and emotional cogency to an over-schematized conception of her character. Clark tends to blame this weakness on Strindberg's influence on O'Neill: "I feel that *Strange Interlude* is not the perfect work it might have been. For one thing, the shade of Strindberg hovers too close over it all: there is something strained, a bit diagrammatic and intellectualized in the character of Nina. She is rather too special - too much the female of the species. If Nina is the inimical Erdgeist, she is at the same time the Earth Mother. Or rather, she ought to be. Woman, the beast of prey, is Strindberg's invention, and I don't think O'Neill's vision of the world is as narrow and warped as that of the Swedish poet." Admittedly, the danger of over-intellectualization, of cerebral abstraction, is present. It is possible, however, to overcome such a danger through subtle, sensitive directing and through a creative interpretation of the role of Nina Leeds by a competent actress. A playwright, it seems hardly necessary to say, is entitled to at least this much in the production of his play.

Question: Discuss O'Neill's use of modern psychological theory in *Strange Interlude*.

Answer: O'Neill's extensive use of the soliloquy and of the aside unheard by the other characters is at once a result of the modern concern with inner states of being and also a dramatic device for probing the consciousness of the characters. The radical shift of emphasis from objective reality to the subjective knower - a crudely oversimplified definition of romanticism - is without a doubt one of the major revolutions in the intellectual, aesthetic history of the West. On all levels of thought and sensibility the major forces and influences of the past two hundred years have combined to create an atmosphere in which man has become more conscious of himself, more aware of the huge, largely uncharted realms of internal experience which play so crucial a role in human existence. Kant, Bergson, Freud, Jung, Dostoyevsky, Kafka, Joyce - the list is endless - have in their several ways fostered a concern with the inner, hidden states of man's psychic life, a life which for many is at least as meaningful and valid as man's external manifestations of the self. The dramatic style known as Expressionism, furthermore, is merely the theatrical symptom of this new emphasis and awareness. O'Neill's interest in Expressionism and his use of masks in his plays represent something more than merely an idly curious experimenting with "gimmicks." Leaving aside the question of the success of O'Neill's experiments in this direction, one must look upon such attempts as one more indication of modern drama's interest in laying bare the gulf that exists between man's externalized thoughts, words, and gestures - his persona - on the one hand, and his internal psychic life on the other. Writing in 1932, O'Neill defended his use of masks as "the freest solution of the modern dramatist's problem as to how - with the greatest possible dramatic clarity and economy of means - he can express those profound hidden conflicts of the mind which the probings of psychology continue to disclose to us."

To borrow a phrase from a contemporary philosopher, this "triumph of subjectivity" of which we have been speaking is nowhere more clearly evident than in the radically revolutionary discoveries and speculations of Sigmund Freud and his many successors. Writing out of an intellectual climate which was excitedly buzzing with the theories and findings of modern psychoanalysis, O'Neill was obviously deeply influenced by the ideas of such men as Freud, Jung, and Adler in many of his plays, most explicitly so in *Strange Interlude*.

Psychoanalytic Theory: A great deal has been written about O'Neill's use of psychoanalytic theory in his plays, including several studies in professional psychiatric journals. One may easily become bogged down in the labyrinthine intricacies of the subject in analyzing the relationship between many of O'Neill's characters, ideas, and symbols, and the corresponding concepts in the literature of modern psychiatry. It is not necessary for our purposes to launch a detailed study of, for example, the similarities between many of O'Neill's characters and the categories of personality types as defined by someone like Karen Horney. It is impossible, however, to ignore the obvious - and to some, obtrusive - presence of Sigmund Freud, and possibly Carl Jung and Alfred Adler, in the pages of *Strange Interlude*. It is more than a question of O'Neill's giving dramatic expression to a general truth promulgated by Freud and restated by one of his contemporary followers, Norman Brown, namely, that "we either come to terms with our unconscious instincts and drives - with life and with death - or else we surely die." Such a statement can, without a doubt, stand as an admirably concise summary of one of the play's central meanings. The whole purpose, in fact, of the sustained tension between spoken thoughts and unspoken asides in this play is to clothe this truth in the flesh and bones of dramatic art. O'Neill's use of Freudian theory is, however, much more extensive and detailed than that.

The Theater Of Tomorrow: Writing in 1921 in *The Theater of Tomorrow*, Kenneth MacGowan, O'Neill's close friend and theatrical associate, prophesied that the play of the future "will attempt to transfer to dramatic art the illumination of those deep and vigorous and eternal processes of the human soul which the psychology of Freud and Jung has given us through the study of the unconscious, striking to the heart of emotion and linking our life today with the emanations of the primitive racial mind." This manifesto-like declaration provides an illuminating gloss on O'Neill's methods and general purposes in *Strange Interlude*. All of the major movements, conflicts, and resolutions of this play are worked out in explicitly Freudian terms. Nina's repressed guilt feelings stemming from her sexual denial of the dead Gordon Shaw, her attempts to punish herself and allay her guilt through her promiscuous sexual conduct at the hospital, her rejection of the father as the authoritarian death figure, her unnaturally possessive attachment to her son - these and more can be cited as instances of O'Neill's deliberate, self-conscious use of Freudian theory in defining the characters and conflicts of the play. Freud's name is, in fact, specifically mentioned at one point in the action. Charles Marsden, who can in no sense be said to speak for O'Neill, comments wryly to himself about the young neurologist, Edmund Darrell, "What is his specialty?... neurologist, I think... I hope not psychoanalyst...a lot to account for, Herr Freud!...punishment to fit his crimes, be forced to listen eternally during breakfast while innumerable plain ones tell him dreams about snakes...pah, what an easy cure-all!...sex the philosopher's stone... 'O Oedipus, O my king! the world is adopting you!'" Ironically, Marsden is here unwittingly voicing one of the truths which emerges from the action of the play. In spite of Marsden's sarcastic skepticism, the world, as O'Neill saw it, is in fact adopting Oedipus and the sexual explanation of human behavior.

O'Neill's Ambivalence: Although Darrell is a neurologist, his speech, diagnoses, and prescriptions are suspiciously like those we would expect of a psychiatrist. His role as the seer, as the semidivine medicine man of modern society, is, however, complex. While his reading of Nina's situation is accurate enough, his prescribed cure proves ultimately disastrous for himself as well as for Nina. This final failure may very well be O'Neill's way of expressing his own skepticism about the omniscience of modern science in general and psychiatry in particular. O'Neill's ambivalent attitude toward the body of doctrine he used so extensively in this play is admirably summed up by Edwin Engel, who speaks of "O'Neill's reiterated moral that it is unwise to meddle in human lives, an argument which would apply, presumably, to the psychoanalyst's efforts to cure mental illness. Darrell is to pay dearly for his meddling." Engel goes on to suggest that "O'Neill did not intend to make of *Strange Interlude* a Freudian tract. Careful to avoid commitments in that regard, he made Darrell a neurologist instead of a psychoanalyst.... As a neurologist Darrell could display a credible familiarity with psychoanalytic theory without injecting into the play immoderate emphasis upon such matters." Speaking of Marsden's contemptuous references to Darrell, Engel argues, "It would be erroneous to assume that Marsden's disdain is O'Neill's praise. In short, O'Neill's position with respect to psychoanalysis is an equivocal one. On the one hand it enriched his knowledge of psychopathology and confirmed his earlier conclusions regarding man's irrational and primitive nature.... On the other hand, O'Neill shut the door in the analyst's face, preferring to let the character wage his own struggle with blind fate."

Facile Freudianism: Whatever one's final judgment as to the validity of the psychoanalytic view of human behavior adopted by O'Neill, several facts stand indisputably clear. The playwright's use of Freudian theory is on the one hand too pat, too facilely simple. It is this apparently unsophisticated exploitation of certain Freudian categories which has led to the condemnation of *Strange Interlude* as "not an original dramatic composition, but a case history." As we have just noted, however, O'Neill's over-all attitude toward the body of psychoanalytic theory he so baldly exploits in this play reveals his reservations about the ultimate validity of that doctrine as an explanation and cure for human unhappiness. In the final analysis, O'Neill seems to be suggesting, nothing can prevent man's nemesis from tragically destroying him. It might be added, finally, that, regardless of one's evaluation of the truth or falsity of the psychological content of the play, the doctrines of Freud, Jung, and others which O'Neill translates into dramatic terms have served the dramatist as an intellectual scaffolding in much the same way that the humor psychology served Shakespeare, Ben Jonson, and their contemporaries in creating the rich dramatic literature of the Elizabethan and Jacobean eras.

Question: Every writer in some way incorporates his view of life - his standards, value judgments and ideas - in his work. To what extent and in what way is this true of Eugene O'Neill's *Strange Interlude*?

Answer: O'Neill's view of the human situation is essentially tragic. Writing out of the agonies of his personal life and strengthened in his tragic view of existence by his readings in the works of such men as Strindberg, Nietzsche, and Schopenhauer, O'Neill created a body of work which in various ways presents man as the victim of an inescapable tragic destiny. The terms in which the dramatist explicates his world view differ from play to play. Sometimes the dramatist's idiom is weighted down with the vocabulary and vision of pessimistic naturalism, sometimes with the apparatus of Greek myth, or the categories of psychoanalysis, or with the outmoded concepts of Christian theology, or in some cases - such as in *Long Day's Journey into Night* - with the intensely personal, agonized details and memories of his own life.

Strange Interlude, as we have seen, is freighted down with Freudian psychology layered over with theological implications and striving to attain to the status of Jungian myth. The view of the human situation which permeates this play can be stated in Freudian terms as the conflict between man's yearning to fulfill the instinctual drives of his pleasure principle and the failure of that yearning to comply with the reality principle. Caught between the Scylla and Charybdis of these contradictory principles, "Man dies and he is not happy," to quote the words of Albert Camus' **protagonist** Caligula, in the play of the same name. Or as Mrs. Evans says to Nina during their dramatic encounter in Act Three, "I used to be a great one for worrying about what's God and what's devil, but I got richly over it living here with poor folks that was being punished for no sins of their own, and me being punished with them for no sin but loving much. Being happy, that's the nearest we can ever come to knowing what's good! Being happy, that's good! The rest is just talk!" Psychoanalytic theory, within its own perspective and in its own terms, has also defined man's tragic dilemma. In the words of a modern disciple of Freud, Norman Brown, in his stimulating study *Life Against Death*, "Freud's writings, taken as a whole, vacillate between two opposite answers to this perpetual question of unhappy humanity. Sometimes the counsel is instinctual renunciation: Grow up and give up your infantile dreams of pleasure, recognize reality for what it is. And sometimes the counsel is instinctual liberation: Change this harsh reality so that you may recover lost sources of pleasure. And sometimes, of course, Freud attempts a compromise between the two attitudes. Thus for example the reality-principle, which he first defined nakedly as an allegiance to 'that which is real, even if it should be unpleasant,' is later softened into that 'which at bottom also seeks pleasure-although a delayed and diminished pleasure, one which is assured by its realization of fact, its relation to reality.' This dilemma explains Freud's drift to pessimism." There in a nutshell, with all the risks of over-simplification, is a definition of the tragic dilemma of Nina Leeds.

Over and above O'Neill's tragic view of life, a view which in *Strange Interlude* has many clearly Freudian resonances, it is possible to detect in this play certain other aspects of the dramatist's world view. A work of art is, it must be remembered, in some mysterious, oblique way, the product of the artist's vision, and that vision is in turn compounded of the values and judgments of the seer. In *Strange Interlude*, for example, there is woven into the dramatic texture of the work many of O'Neill's judgments and views of modern society.

The Playwright's Values: Examining the characters in the order of their appearance, we find embodied in them many of the playwright's strictures against certain inadequate or false views held by many in our time. Professor Leeds, for example, by his retreat into the safety and moral security of a scholarly study of the past, has given up the struggle which living in the present implies and demands. In fact, to put it more accurately, he has never even taken up that struggle in the first place. The tragic repetition of this failure is revealed in his daughter's inability to grapple with the present. She attempts to exist in a land of fantasy bounded on the one side by bitter memory and on the other by futile hope. As she says to herself, "The only living life is in the past and future…the present is an interlude…strange interlude in which we call on past and future to bear witness we are living." Her father, significantly, emerges out of his antiseptic world only to meddle selfishly in the present by preventing her marriage to Gordon. As he himself confesses to Nina, "Let us say then that I persuaded myself it was for your sake. That may be true. You are young. You think one can live with truth. Very well. It is also true I was jealous of Gordon. I was alone and I wanted to keep your love. I hated him as one hates a thief one may not accuse nor punish. I did my best to prevent your marriage. I was glad when he died." O'Neill is clearly saying that the way of Professor Leeds is the way of death. It is no accident that Act One closes with the anticipation of his death and Act Two opens on the fact of his death.

Marsden's Retreat: Charles Marsden, ex-student of Professor Leeds, friend of the family, Nina's constant lover, is another pathetic figure who attempts to escape the realities of the present by flight into the controllable world of art. But just as the Professor's scholarship was a false and sterile scholarship, so too is Marsden's art a false and sterile art. It is in the nature of neither scholarship nor art to afford a psychic haven for those too timorous to face the world of harsh actuality. In both cases these men, Leeds and Marsden, have prostituted their calling. O'Neill's indictment of Marsden is openly stern and condemnatory, possibly because this insipid writer of genteel literature was fouling the nest that O'Neill himself had chosen to inhabit.

Inadequacy Of Science: In the case of Ned Darrell, the attractive young doctor who falls in love with Nina, calculatingly fathers her child, and comes close to being destroyed by his involvement with her, the dramatist's attitude is more complex than in the case of Leeds and Marsden. O'Neill's own interest in psychoanalysis obviously led him to see a good deal of value in the insights and ministrations of one who is, like Darrell, the spokesman for this new science. As a replacement for an absent God and a lost sense of values, however, the psychoanalytic explanation of the human predicament must, as O'Neill views it, eventually prove unsatisfactory. This seems to be implied in so far as Darrell's prescriptions for happiness become destructively meddlesome acts. A further hammering home of this judgment can be inferred from Darrell's becoming a research biologist in a remote station, where the only life he can ever meddle with again is single-celled. One is reminded of O'Neill's letter to George Jean Nathan, quoted earlier, in which the dramatist wrote of his wish to "dig at the roots of the sickness of today as I feel it - the death of the old God and failure of science and materialism to give any satisfactory new one...."

Emptiness Of Financial Success: The same passage from O'Neill's letter to Nathan also provides a clue to the playwright's attitude toward Sam Evans, the man who, by contemporary standards, is the one successful figure in the play. He has amassed a fortune, married a beautiful woman, and raised a son who is destined, it seems, to repeat the successes of his father. The house is built upon sand, however, since the beautiful woman has never really loved him and the son is not his own. The hollowness of Sam Evans' life is indicated by the fact that the most important thing in his life seems to be his son's winning his final collegiate varsity race. O'Neill neither sneers nor fulminates; he merely presents. His indictment of what Sam Evans stands for is, on the whole, implicit. And yet this successful business tycoon, it must be pointed out, is not tormented and twisted by inner yearnings, fears, and resentments, as are his two partner-rivals, Marsden and Darrell. It is undoubtedly because he is too adolescently simple-minded to be much bothered by the agonies which the repressive forces of modern civilization have impose on the sensitive. It is almost - but not quite - as if O'Neill is looking back nostalgically to a life of pastoral innocence and mourning the loss of the simple, quiet life. Sam, it will be recalled, grew up close to the land as a farmer. There is in O'Neill's depiction of this man a note of ambivalence. Sam Evans is, if you like, one of the last of the primitives.

The playwright, as we have seen, in creating Professor Leeds, Charles Marsden, Edmund Darrell, and Sam Evans, is molding his characters out of his own private vision of what man is, what he should be, and what he can and cannot be. These characters are, in varying ways, clearly the products of Eugene O'Neill's standards, judgments, and values. They could not have been otherwise.

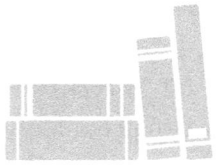

SELECTED BIBLIOGRAPHY

The O'Neill bibliography is vast and grows vaster by the day. What follows, consequently, is no more than a preliminary guide to a few of the basic works. Those interested in extended research on O'Neill should consult several basic bibliographies listing works by and about O'Neill. The first is *A Bibliography of the Works of Eugene O'Neill* by Ralph Sanborn and Barrett H. Clark, 1931. The second is Jackson R. Bryer's "Forty Years of O'Neill Criticism: A Selected Bibliography," published in the periodical *Modern Drama*, IV, 2, Sept. 1961, pp. 196–216. A third bibliography is Jordan Y. Miller's *Eugene O'Neill and the American Critic*, 1962. There is also a splendid selected bibliography appended to the volume of critical essays edited by Oscar Cargill and listed below.

EDITIONS OF THE PLAY

Strange Interlude, Boni and Liveright, New York, 1928.

Nine Plays, Introduction by Joseph Wood Krutch, Liveright, New York, 1932. This collection was reissued by Random House as a Modern Library edition, 1954.

The Plays of Eugene O'Neill, Vol. I, Random House, New York, 1941, 1951.

BIOGRAPHY

Gelb, Arthur, and Barbara Gelb. *O'Neill*, 1960. This 970-page study is an absorbingly readable chronicle of the life and works of the playwright. A storehouse of information, it has become the standard biography.

Clark, Barrett H. *Eugene O'Neill*, 1926. Revised several times under the title *Eugene O'Neill: The Man and His Plays*. Written by a friend and longtime admirer, the book contains a good deal of firsthand information and letters as well as critical comments on the individual plays. It was revised and brought up to date in 1947.

CRITICAL STUDIES: GENERAL BOOKS

Cargil, Oscar, ed. *O'Neill and His Plays*, 1961. This intelligently selected collection of essays on the man and on the works is probably the single most valuable compendium of O'Neill criticism.

Gassner, John, ed. *O'Neill: A Collection of Critical Essays*, 1964. A slender but valuable selection, including a balanced critical appraisal of O'Neill's achievement by the editor.

Engel, Edwin A. *The Haunted Heroes of Eugene O'Neill*, 1953. A study of the plays, including a provocative analysis of *Strange Interlude*. Engel traces recurring **themes** in the plays.

Falk, Doris V. *Eugene O'Neill and the Tragic Tension*, 1958. Heavily weighted in the direction of psychoanalysis, the author's studies of the individual plays are brief but usually stimulating. Her analysis of *Strange Interlude* is little more than a summary.

Carpenter, Frederic I. *Eugene O'Neill*, 1964. Traces a pattern running through O'Neill's plays in terms of the dramatist's life.

There are, of course, scores of other works devoted wholly or in part to a study of O'Neill's work. In addition to the books mentioned above there are individual chapters in the following works which merit special attention:

Brustein, Robert. *The Theater of Revolt*, 1964.

Krutch, Joseph Wood. *American Drama Since 1918*, 1939.

Gassner, John. *Masters of the Drama*, 1954.

Quinn, Arthur Hobson. *A History of the American Drama*, 1937.

ESSAYS AND ARTICLES: GENERAL

An entire issue of *Modern Drama*, III, 3, December 1960, was given over to a study of O'Neill's work. The essays include specialized studies on the influence of Hindu mysticism on O'Neill's work, his use of dialogue, and the comic spirit in his plays, as well as more general studies. Most of the important articles and essays on O'Neill have been reprinted in the Cargill and Gassner collections listed above. The student of O'Neill's work might also be interested in consulting a two-part survey of the O'Neill criticism which has given special emphasis to the psychological elements in the plays:

Nethercot, Arthur A. "The Psychoanalyzing of Eugene O'Neill," *Modern Drama*, III, 3, December 1960, and III, 4, February 1961.

SPECIAL STUDIES OF STRANGE INTERLUDE

Excerpts from the reviews of the original 1928 production are reprinted in the Gelbs' biography of O'Neill, pp. 659–62. In addition to the analyses of the plays found in the books by Clark, Krutch, Engel, Falk, and Carpenter (all listed above), the interested reader may want to look at the following studies of the play:

Alexander, Doris M. "*Strange Interlude* and Schopenhauer," *American Literature*, XXV, May 1953.

Battenhouse, Roy W. "*Strange Interlude* Restudied," *Religion in Life*, XV, Spring 1946.

Gillet, Louis. "La clef des songes" *Revue des deux Mondes* XLIX, January 1929.

Malone, Kemp, "The **Diction** of *Strange Interlude*," *American Speech*, VI, October 1930.

Montgomery, Guy. "*Strange Interlude*," *University of California Chronicles*, XXX, July 1928.

www.ingramcontent.com/pod-product-compliance
Lightning Source LLC
LaVergne TN
LVHW011713060526
838200LV00051B/2886